ONE FOOT OUT THE DOOR

ONE FOOT OUT THE DOOR

HOW TO COMBAT
THE PSYCHOLOGICAL RECESSION
THAT'S ALIENATING EMPLOYEES
AND HURTING AMERICAN BUSINESS

Judith M. Bardwick, Ph.D.

AMACOM American Management Association
New York | Atlanta | Brussels | Chicago | Mexico City | San Francisco
Shanghai | Tokyo | Toronto | Washington, D. C.

This publication is designed to provide accurate and authoritative information in regard to the subject matter covered. It is sold with the understanding that the publisher is not engaged in rendering legal, accounting, or other professional service. If legal advice or other expert assistance is required, the services of a competent professional person should be sought.

Library of Congress Cataloging-in-Publication Data

Bardwick, Judith M., 1933–
    One foot out the door : how to combat the psychological recession that's alienating employees and hurting American business / Judith M. Bardwick.
        p.   cm.
    Includes index.
    ISBN 978-0-8144-8058-8
    1. Psychology, Industrial—United States.   2. Employees—United States—Attitudes.   3. Employee morale—United States.   4. Management—Psychological aspects.   5. Quality of work life—United States.   I. Title.   II. Title: Psychological recession that's alienating employees and hurting American business.   III. Title: Recession that's alienating employees and hurting American business.

    HF5548.8.B2435 2007
    658.3′14—dc22

                                                                                    2007020973

Printing number

10 9 8 7 6 5 4 3 2 1

This book is for
Captain Allen E. Armstrong, USCG, Retired
to the man and his life
in loving memory

CONTENTS

■ CHAPTER 6

COMMITMENT AND ENGAGEMENT— *NOT* MORALE OR SATISFACTION   63

■ CHAPTER 7

CREATE SIGNIFICANT RELATIONSHIPS BETWEEN BOSSES AND SUBORDINATES   77

■ CHAPTER 13

PSYCHOLOGY IS MORE
IMPORTANT THAN ECONOMICS   189

ACKNOWLEDGMENTS

I wanted the authorship of this book to read, *"by* Judith M. Bardwick *with* Stephen R. Hardis." Steve Hardis, whose corporate experience enriches this book in many ways, is my brother. He wouldn't let me give him co-author credit. "No, Judy," he said, "this is your book." But his contribution to the book is enormous. He brings an extraordinary depth of experience, insight, eloquence, and a sense of humanity that made these issues and solutions much clearer and more vivid. My love and admiration for my brother are immense. *Many* thanks, Steve.

My long-time personal team is made up of four extraordinary women. Of the four, three of us have worked together for many years: my administrator, Helen Bloomfield, a person of vast knowledge and skills; Adrienne Hickey, AMACOM's senior acquisition editor (recently retired), who is the most discerning editor I have ever met; and Maggie Stuckey, my working editor, who somehow manages to get inside my head and organizes my ideas and expresses my thoughts better than I do. New to the team is Laurie Harper, a marvelous literary agent who negotiated a contract that pleased both AMACOM and me in equal measure, which is no small feat.

Special thanks are due to James K. Clifton of the Gallup Organization, Gallup Worldwide, and WatsonWyatt, who allowed me to include the results of their extremely valuable research.

Producing a book is a complicated process with challenging deadlines. It requires expertise and collaboration among everyone involved in getting the ideas and words right, getting it on paper and between covers and into stores, and making sure the world knows there's a new book they really ought to read. Many thanks to the AMACOM team, without which none of that could have happened:

Christina Parisi, the new acquisitions editor who picked up the reins from Adrienne; managing editor Andy Ambraziejus; Irene Majuk, publicity director; Cathleen Ouderkirk, creative director; Jenny Wesselmann, marketing director; and Therese Mausser, director of subsidiary and international rights. To all I express my gratitude.

CHAPTER ONE

TOPSY-TURVY:
THE SKY IS FALLING!

OR MOST OF THE TWENTIETH CENTURY, American businesses were fat, dumb, and happy. American products dominated their industries, corporate treasuries were rich, and the word "global" was never heard outside third-grade geography classrooms.

Of course, many companies were brought to their knees during the 1930s, but then World War II changed everything. The American economy took off on a spectacular trajectory that dominated for decades.

American businesses had no real competition. The same two oceans that had protected us from military invasion also protected us from economic competition. In addition, the industrial infrastructure of Japan and much of Europe had been destroyed during the war. While they struggled to rebuild, American economic dominance soared.

In this period of American hegemony, large American

firms enjoyed what amounted to monopolistic status. We had real monopolies like AT&T, de facto monopolies like IBM, Xerox®, and Kodak, and psychological monopolies (companies that acted like monopolies even though they were not) like GM and Ford.

And the people who worked there enjoyed what amounted to lifetime job security. This was especially true in unionized industries. Generally speaking, companies agreed with unions that rising prices were not a major concern and rising wages were a good thing. But this expectation of permanent job security was not limited to union workers. Among American workers, there was a universal belief that unless you screwed up in a major way, you had a job for life.

It was nothing less than a social contract, albeit often implied, between worker and employer. In this contract, employees agreed to work hard, and employers agreed to take care of them. The workers became the primary stakeholders of the organization.

Companies fed this expectation by focusing on employee welfare. Morale surveys were required in almost every large organization, and woe to any manager whose employees said they were unhappy or dissatisfied. The basic premise was that if organizations were very generous to employees, employees would be happy and therefore productive—and not tempted to join unions.

It was a successful strategy for many years; so successful that companies were caught by surprise when the world started to change.

THE WORLD TURNED UPSIDE DOWN

It began in the late 1970s, when imported products from Germany and Japan, such as cars and electronics, outsold American products, even in the United States, because of better quality and more competitive prices. For the first time since the end of World War II, the largely monopolistic status of large American firms was threatened. Although monopolies like AT&T were hit with federal antitrust challenges, it was really the borderless economy that changed everything.

After so many years of being at the top and taking that status for granted, U.S. CEOs were completely unprepared for worldwide competition, and they panicked. The global economy was developing all around them, and its implications were not yet understood. So for approximately 10 to 15 years, managers flailed about, trying every new guru offering and technological innovation. But the key measure of corporate success—share price—kept slipping.

> After so many years of being at the top, U.S. CEOs were completely unprepared for worldwide competition, and they panicked.

Under increasing pressure from Wall Street and threatened by corporate raiders, CEOs became ever more desperate to save their companies. Eventually, they decided the most effective strategy to improve the share price would be to bring costs down, thereby increasing profits. One obvious place to cut costs was the workforce. That's when management decided to break the implied social contract of respecting employees as key stakeholders.

We all know what happened next: massive cutbacks, layoffs, restructuring, downsizing, rightsizing, and outsourcing. Euphemisms abounded, but the harsh reality was that many people saw their jobs vanish; many, many others felt vulnerable.

Even those who still had jobs felt threatened, as corporations reached deeper in their search for cost cutting. Over time, health care benefits for employees and their dependents were cut, or workers had to assume more of the cost, or both; pensions were reorganized, tightened, restructured, or abolished altogether.

Thus, in a relatively short period, people saw their entire economic structure crumble. Job security, long taken for granted, disappeared. The benefits that provided security for the family shriveled. And, with greatly increased competition, the presumption that wages should keep rising could no longer be defended. The result was that people lost all three: job security, family safety nets, and the certainty of a gradual incremental rise in their standard of living.

Many people in many parts of the world, who had enjoyed the security of a job with one employer for their entire working life and lifelong freedom from economic risk, lost it all. In many nations, in many organizations, in a range of industries, occupations, and professions, job and thus life security were either gone or in jeopardy. Too much job security had been replaced by too little.

By the 1980s workers were no longer the key stakeholders in American businesses. The only stakeholder that really mattered was the shareholder, and the price of a company's stock became the only meaningful measure of success or failure. The pendulum of social values had swung in a wide arc.

THE CRAZY 1990S

At about the same time, another seismic shift was developing.

The last major recession occurred in 1981–1982. After that, for roughly the next 20 years (except for the minor recession of 1991), the economy continued to grow, and so did optimism and expectations. For almost 20 years, practically the length of a generation, normality meant an economy with unlimited opportunities and little downside, especially for educated people with valuable skills and talents.

Millionaires on paper were (almost) a dime a dozen. Employees of high-tech companies, especially those who had joined the organization when it was just a start-up, had seven-

and eight-figure stock portfolios as soon as they cashed in their options. Hundreds of thousands of people, mostly young and well educated, found themselves far richer than they ever imagined possible. How heady it was!

Stephen Hardis, former CEO of the Eaton Corporation, recently observed, "This generation expected to get rich quickly and saw evidence all around them that these were reasonable expectations. They were courted; they did not get interviewed as much as they interviewed outfits that might be lucky enough to hire them. It was an era when HR folks preached 'there is a war on for talent' and options and signing bonuses were given out as if they had no cost. This was particularly relevant in the emerging technology areas, where the cost of doing business was considered inconsequential when the objective was to gain size (scale) and share price as quickly as possible."[1]

All of us remember the thrilling mantra of the 1990s: the "New Economy." With the turn of a phrase, all the old rules of prudent investment and management—diversification, dividends, profitability—were replaced by business models that assumed their concepts, alone, would create success and prosperity. It was no longer necessary, in the view of the "new economy," to build a successful enterprise.

In the new economy, old rules were a major impediment and only old fogies stuck with the New York Stock Exchange. Those who "got it" rushed to Nasdaq, and the "real players" quit their jobs to become day traders.

CNN, FOX, and CNBC filled every 24 hours with talking heads describing the breakthrough of the worldwide economy and money that could speed through a wireless world in a nanosecond. Then, in a media-driven echo effect, the idea would get picked up by *The Wall Street Journal, Fortune, Business Week,* and more, and ultimately it would be on the front page of every local newspaper's business section, because no one wants to be left behind, the only dinosaur in a universe of space travel in which the only real impediment is too little imagination to leave the past back where it belongs and move, with giant steps, into the unimaginable new economy.

COLLAPSE

Then, in the spring of 2001, it all started unraveling. The boom collapsed, as booms inevitably do, Nasdaq pretty much died, and the dot-coms disappeared into the hole of naïve failure. As odd as it seems in retrospect, most people were truly shocked. The echo effect, and their temporary paper wealth, had wiped out their reservoir of appropriate skepticism.

Employees at every level in a huge range of industries were by then horribly familiar with large lay-offs and prolonged unemployment. Imports and outsourcing had displaced a number of the higher-paying American jobs, and unions, stuck in an old time warp, were ineffective at developing new strategies to increase the welfare of their members.

But what was particularly stunning is what happened to the young elite of the 1990s—the poster children of guaranteed success.

THE SPECIAL CASE OF THE BEST
AND BRIGHTEST

For sheer symbolism of unexpected economic vulnerability, consider what happened to the educated, ambitious, and hard-working Best and Brightest: technology wizards in telecoms and wireless companies; financial services professionals, especially investment bankers; top executives and professionals of defunct dot-coms; and the liberal arts majors who graduated at the top of their classes and flocked to creative jobs in media or music or fashion.[2] Following the stock market bust and the imploding of the dot-com bubble, they went from being courted by employers to being unemployable for as long as five years.

- Robert was a successful young engineer who specialized in CadCam blueprints. His job went overseas. He is now working as a farrier.
- Lorne was a head of a branch of an international bank. He directed 20 people who made loans to the movie industry. After the bank closed its Los Angeles branch, he became a house-husband.
- Sarah was a Wall Street bond trader who earned $1 million a year in salary and bonus. She now works on commission only.
- John was a CFO who went from Wall Street to dot-com start-ups. After the dot-coms disappeared, there was no venture capital money and he was out of work for three years.

Here is a personal observation of this phenomenon. In the spring of 2003, our daughter-in-law and two-and-a-half-year-old granddaughter came to visit. As we live in San Diego, this meant trips to Sea World, LegoLand, and the famous zoo. It was midweek, not a holiday, and the parks were filled. They were filled with young children, of course, but what really surprised me was who accompanied the children—not babysitters, but parents. Most of these adults were in their thirties and early forties, with obvious signs of affluence: expert haircuts, stylish clothes, gym-hardened bodies, and dressed-up toddlers in very expensive baby buggies. And at least one-third of these adults were men. These parents were in the park because they were not in the labor force.

Unemployment is only one manifestation of economic recession, but it is the one that causes the most pain to individual workers and their families. Looking at the big picture, economists might say that things were not so bad right then. The unemployment rate of just under six percent at that time was actually historically moderate, but that was of little comfort to the unemployed, and it was especially bitter for people who never expected to be vulnerable—highly educated, very successful professionals and members of management. They were disproportionately affected by worldwide economic conditions and especially hard hit by prolonged unemployment.

So the most valued employees of the 1990s became the least employable by the turn of the century. As the tech boom crashed, investors stopped investing and the glamour industries laid people off instead of hiring them.

They never saw it coming.

> The most valued employees of the 1990s became the least employable by the turn of the century.

These people were the winners, the "high-potentials," in the halcyon days in which they grew up, went to school, and entered the labor force. And now, they were the hardest hit by the recession. Faced with continued unemployment, many in this group (aged roughly 22 to 47 in 2007) have dashed expectations, crushed confidence, and bewilderment about what to do next. *"I was a project manager [or head of sales, chief engineer, CEO, COO, CFO, CTO] and now I'm out of work and no one's returning my calls."*

This is particularly important from a macroeconomic perspective because the standard response to what individuals need to do to stay employed is *education, education and education.* After the 1990s bust, many of our best-educated and highly skilled people could not find jobs for as long as five years.[3]

- Educated workers were especially prone to bouts of long-term unemployment in this downturn.
- These workers often have specific, especially technical, skills, so it sometimes took them longer to find a job that matched their experience and education.
- In the downturn, their skills were not needed because their industries were retrenching or failing in the postbust economy.
- Of the 1.9 million workers who were unemployed for six months or more from 2001 to 2003, one in five was a former executive, professional, or manager.

If education isn't the answer, what is? In the long term, education is the answer, but in the short term, a financial cushion, or a working partner, and personal resilience are what's needed.

RECOVERY AND PRODUCTIVITY

In the years since the recession of 2001, American companies have made their way back to profitability, some by leaps and some by inches. With few exceptions, the gains are the result of increased productivity—fewer people doing more. Since 2001, average productivity has increased five percent annually.

Increased productivity is a good thing—as long as you're not the one whose job disappeared. It showed up first in a broad swath of manufacturing industries, after manufacturers made major investments in new technologies and new equipment. Now the service businesses, which constitute 80 percent of our economy, such as retail, transportation and finance, are cutting jobs and increasing sales.

In 2003, in the middle of the economic recovery, there were still massive job cuts. The number of "discouraged workers," people who want to work but have given up looking, was approximately 9.2 million and the number who were working part-time because they couldn't get full-time jobs was up to 4.8 million.[4] While it became fashionable and politically correct to point to outsourcing to lower-wage nations as the culprit behind the lack of job growth, the real cause was the drive for higher rates of productivity.[5]

This has become acutely obvious in recent years in the operations of private-equity firms, which have emerged in the last decade as a major new phenomenon.[6] Using many of the same techniques as corporate raiders during the leveraged buyout era of the 1980s, these firms have emerged as among the most successful and aggressive acquirers of business. Because they don't have the same pressure to achieve short-term results as publicly held companies do, they can restructure organizations more aggressively despite the immediate negative effect that has on earnings.

Just like the corporate raiders of the earlier LBO era, private-equity groups in the twenty-first century discern and purchase unrealized equity and are a threat to complacent management. But, again like the earlier corporate raiders, they are also a threat to the average employee because their goal is to achieve a very high rate of return within five years or less. The most popular way to do this? Cut jobs to drive down costs. Private-equity groups are not in the business of growing organizations and creating jobs.

Today, the American economy, measured in real dollars and cents, is actually strong and getting stronger (see Chapter 11 for a plethora of evidence). By 2005, the economy had grown so much that job growth had begun in earnest and continued through 2006. Yet it doesn't *seem* that way to American workers. The explanation for this apparent contradiction lies in the realm of psychology, which is the topic of the next chapter.

> Today, the American economy, measured in real dollars and cents, is actually strong and getting stronger. Yet it doesn't *seem* that way to American workers.

Despite the evidence, too many Americans, one by one by one, have a general perception that things are not going well and that their families could stumble into disaster at any time. When we add together all the fears and worries of all the individuals, what we have is a widespread sense of vulnerability in the American workplace.

This is disastrous for businesses. People who are perpetually fearful have lost the wherewithal to do their best work. This crippling psychological condition may be the most lasting and most damaging result of the rise of globalism.

How do we combat this crippling condition? The answer is twofold.

First, leaders of America's businesses need to open their eyes, recognize the symptoms, and take organizational action. The later chapters of this book lay out a game plan of interventions that will overcome apathy and fear and replace them with a spirit of engagement and commitment.

The second is larger. As a nation, we need to reinstate people's confidence in the country and in their future. To shift these paralyzing attitudes, people must have a balanced view of how the economy is actually doing, rather than how it *seems* to be doing.

With about half of our citizens feeling naked and abandoned by their companies, the nation needs a twenty-first-century safety net that will reduce the fear by providing financial support and a sense of community, while avoiding a reinstatement of entitlement attitudes.

Obviously, business leaders have a major role to play in shifting public attitudes and establishing a safety net. But they cannot do it alone. It requires courage, clear thinking, and real leadership from national decision makers.

These are big questions, and they are tackled in the final three chapters of this book. In those chapters, readers will find financial evidence of the strength of the economy, an outline of a three-legged safety net, and observations on what we need from our nation's leaders, today and into the future.

The need is urgent. After many decades of being fat, dumb, and happy, American businesses and American workers have been forced into change. In a relatively short time, fat has morphed into thin and happy into frightened. Prolonged fear does not bode well for future success.

CHAPTER TWO

THE PSYCHOLOGICAL
RECESSION

A NOT-SO-FUNNY THING HAPPENED on the way to the twenty-first century: people stopped caring about their jobs.

Until relatively recently, the most important stakeholders in American organizations were the employees. They came to work each day with commitment, loyalty, even passion, and, because they sensed that the company felt the same commitment toward them, they gave it their all.

Now, after years of downsizing, outsourcing, and a cavalier corporate attitude that treats employees as costs rather than assets, most of today's workers have concluded that the company no longer values them. So they, in turn, no longer feel engaged in their work or committed to the company. The reality of mutual codependence between employees and organizations, and the advantages gained from long-term mutual commitment and engagement, have been lost.

As many as two-thirds of U.S. employees are either actively looking for new jobs or merely going through the motions at their current jobs. While they still show up for work each day, in the ways that really count, many have quit. Figuratively, and in some cases literally, they already have one foot out the door.

They are afflicted with a condition I call the Psychological Recession. It is an emotional state in which people feel extremely vulnerable and afraid for their futures. It is especially relevant in the business world because chronically fearful people are too exhausted to be creative and innovative. They expect the worst to happen, so they see no reason to give their all.

HOW TO RECOGNIZE A PSYCHOLOGICAL RECESSION

A Psychological Recession, a dour view of the present and an even bleaker view of the future, is a natural outcome to a deep and sustained sense of vulnerability. Once established, this negative mindset reinforces people's view that the world is a risky place in which they have little or no control. In this way, the Psychological Recession feeds on itself. It increases people's fears and their aversion to risk.

There are real issues to worry about: the war in Iraq and terrorism; the fearsome outcome of the spread of a militant and radical form of Islam; rising energy prices and our continued dependence on foreign oil; and, perhaps worst of all, the very visible and widespread loss of job security.

For most people, the issue of job security is the mother lode of anxiety poisoning their view of reality. They have seen, or heard about, or read about, the people who have been laid off, through no fault of their own, and they are terrified they may be next. Economic hard times initially had an impact on hourly workers, but then the impact spread to well-educated knowledge workers. As tax receipts fell, even government workers faced cuts in their ranks. Everyone knows someone who has been affected.

This sense of helpless vulnerability is heightened by the onslaught of news stories about the juggernaut economies of China and India and about our increasing lack of competitiveness in our education systems and businesses. This deep mood of pessimism shouts, *We are doomed!*

Labor is strangely quiet. The unemployment rate over the last five years has averaged five percent or lower, which generally means labor is becoming scarce and thus more valuable. That, in times past, would result in an increase in worker militancy and high demands. Yet there has been almost no response to cuts in jobs or benefits to those employed and retired. In all likelihood, members of organized labor, like everyone else, are paralyzed by their deep feeling of vulnerability to a loss of jobs.

Sustained fear makes people cautious, and that includes our leaders. Governments—municipal, state, and federal—seem unable to protect people in general and from international competition for jobs specifically. Voter apathy is widespread; people see both parties as uninvolved in their welfare and powerless to help. Simultaneously, stories about corporate corruption and church

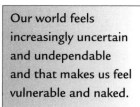

Our world feels increasingly uncertain and undependable and that makes us feel vulnerable and naked.

sex scandals rock our belief and trust in the other major institutions we depend on.

Overall, the public perceives the country's leadership, both political and social, as ineffective, frightened, and impotent. This reinforces people's perception that there's no help to be found anywhere; in the midst of chaos, no one's in charge.

Our world feels increasingly uncertain and undependable and that makes us feel vulnerable and naked. In the search for answers, some have turned to fundamentalist religions. Others have sought comfort in defining the enemies: free trade, technology, NAFTA, legal and illegal immigrants, Wal-Mart, unions, corporations . . . a specific enemy is relatively comforting balanced against an amorphous sense of dread.

The psychological downturn is far worse than the 2001 economic slowdown, and its cause is not explained by outside factors like media bias or bickering between impotent "leaders."[1] This sense of pessimism is rooted in the profound and sustained feelings of vulnerability that many people are experiencing. Anxiety, depression, and a sense of being powerless are a poisonous mix.

This depressive and fearful view, which embraces a permanently half-empty glass, is now held even by many successful employed people. Clearly, skepticism and pessimism have replaced the euphoric optimism of the 1990s boom. Many people, especially those in their twenties, thirties, and forties, feel cheated and scared by the bad luck of hard times. Giving people little or no hope that their lives will embody the American Dream of upward mobility is both stupid and politically dangerous.

A PSYCHOLOGICAL RECESSION IS SELF-FULFILLING

Faced with the reality of a reasonably sudden but permanent loss of economic security, the nation has been gripped by a sense of dread. What started as a feeling of economic vulnerability has generalized into a deep, pervasive fear that there's no way for anyone to make themselves safe because there seems to be no way to regain control over what's happening to them.

Feeling this way, people become preoccupied with trying to make sense out of the chaos of their lives, as if by understanding it, they could somehow control it. But it doesn't work, and it never will work, and here's why. Paradoxically, people who are profoundly scared seek out worst-case examples because that confirms their world view and gives them a sense, however fleeting, that they were right about *something*. The prolonged, sustained fear that is characteristic of a Psychological Recession assures that good news will be discounted while bad news is accepted as the stuff of reality.

The tragedy is that focusing on fears only reinforces them. In understandable but irrational ways, people who are frightened move ever forward toward panic. In this way, a Psychological Recession is self-fulfilling.

The media barrage of bad news doesn't help. The same "echo effect" that contributed to the boom of the 1990s is now having the reverse impact by reinforcing today's gloomy scenario. Somehow, all television stations end up playing the same video of the same plant that was closed, the same workers who were laid off, the same children whose school was closed, the same contract to outsource work to India or China . . . and the loop of information plays endlessly. When the same message is trumpeted, debated, illustrated, and referred to by "experts," the convergence of the cacophony of its echoes makes it "a fact." The notion that something might be just a possibility or inference or idea or opinion is transformed through obsessive, pervasive repetition into a certainty.

The discourse of threat and gloom is never challenged, which only ratchets upward the self-fulfilling nature of the phenomenon.

PERCEPTION VERSUS REALITY

Today, feelings of being alone and vulnerable are proving more powerful in shaping people's attitudes than the actual facts. Over the last five years, the American economy has sustained a strong recovery, with an average annual growth rate of three to five percent. Interest rates are low, unemployment is low, inflation rates are low. Still, Americans are gloomy.

> Greed should be trumping fear, yet it's not. Reality has been nullified by exaggerated, irrational fear.

Greed should be trumping fear, yet it's not. Reality has been nullified by exaggerated, irrational fear. At the very time that the strong recovery should have led to confidence and pride in America's ability to thrive despite ongoing chaos, increasing competition, and threats, instead the American people have lost confidence in their leaders, in institutions, and even in the nation.

How to explain this? In part, it's the difference between national averages, which are vague and amorphous, and individual reality, which is anything but. While the national figures are very positive, many individuals have good reasons to be gloomy: slow growth in wages; benefits increasingly at risk; the insurgency in Iraq and the never-ending possibility of terrorism at home; corporate and government malfeasance; and job growth slower than gains in productivity, which means employers don't need to hire more people to meet increased demand.

People are always astute about what is happening to *them*. While they may feel unexpectedly wealthy because of their homes' appreciation or the general recovery of the stock market (today's average investor is a middle-class person with a household income of about $65,000), everyone who has a job in a successful large company knows that neither annual increases nor their jobs are guaranteed. Similarly, anyone who owns a small business is aware that increasing competition from many sources is a permanent state of affairs.

Still, given the fact that the overall economy is healthy, the widespread view that it's doing poorly now and the future will be worse is far more a matter of perception than of fact. In March 2004, the American Research Group found that 44 percent of people polled believed the country was still in a recession —even though the last recession ended in November of 2001 and was followed by an annualized growth rate of 6.1 percent, the fastest in 20 years.[2]

The media have certainly played a major role in the glass-is-half-empty view; the Media Research Center reported that in August 2005, 62 percent of the news stories on the three main TV networks portrayed the economy in a negative light and negative stories on the economy outweighed positive stories by four to one.[3]

This apparent contradiction between a humming national economy and a widespread sense of foreboding in individuals is easy to understand when we look at it from the perspective of psychology. People are simply anticipating the terrible things that could happen to them, and their absorption with their vulnerability increases the sense of being alone and defenseless. In this way, psychologists are far more relevant in terms of explaining the narrow range of today's stock indexes than are economists.

WHO IS AFFECTED?

Everyone. The impact of a Psychological Recession is more widespread than most people realize because nearly everyone personally knows people who have been directly affected. The result is that even those who are still working are anxious and fearful. They watch their former colleagues, especially the "golden ones," struggle through months or even years of unemployment. They see their companies continuing to downsize, use temps and outsource, and they're afraid they may be next. Stress is everywhere, and it is unrelenting.

At the same time, work itself has become a major source of tension, because when costs must be lowered, the arithmetic of higher productivity means that more work has to be accomplished by fewer and fewer people. This translates to longer work hours for everyone who has a job.

But it's not simply a question of overwork, of too many hours. When people are anxious at work, they're afraid that no amount of effort is good enough. To make themselves safe, they work very hard at everything. They don't feel secure enough, and therefore are not courageous enough, to differentiate among tasks and set priorities. When every task is treated as enormously important, work never ends. There's no closure, no sense of satisfaction of a job well done. People on permanent overload are exhausted, and exhaustion is not a prescription for treating fear and anxiety.

Even more fundamental to our sense of stress is the fact that we have gone from too much (unearned) security to too little. Most people now feel that, even though their performance is excellent and their skills are germane, they have little chance of earning job security. While economies, organizations, and customers are benefiting because of the economy's competitiveness, many individuals are newly vulnerable and downwardly mobile in a world in which work migrates because much of it can be done anywhere.

The effects are widespread. There is confusion and tension at work and at home. In many families, traditional gender roles have moved closer to a unisex model of shared responsibilities, with no one having any real downtime. And, while the pressure at work has grown as organizations are squeezing out every possible percentage increase in productivity, it is harder and harder to find excellent child care. There seems to be no rest for the weary! Technology, in the meantime, has created a boundaryless world in which everyone is reachable, at any time, wherever they happen to be.

Not surprisingly, the Psychological Recession lies especially heavy among the young baby boomers and GenXers, who came of age at the height of the good times and launched their careers believing there were no limits. Today, many of these young and educated people are in denial or in despair, convinced theirs is a lost generation. Some have become waiters and waitresses, doing pick-up jobs that need little training or education, some returned to school, and others went home to mom and dad.[4]

> The Psychological Recession lies especially heavy among the young baby boomers and GenXers.

A generation whose members had the highest expectations and believed in the value of their education has become cynical and depressed. No wonder the mood is one of despair. If the future is dour for them, the future is bleak for all.

WHY IT MATTERS

We all know the mantra:

Get profits up.

How?

By cutting costs.

What's the biggest cost?

Salaries, benefits, pensions, vacations, training, sick days . . . anything to do with people.

What can you do?

End long-term commitments to employees and downsize, lay off, outsource and use temps. Wall Street rewards it, and shareholders are happy.

That's very appealing and logical in the short term. But, in the longer term, not seeing employees as stakeholders and not making a commitment to them is a truly dumb strategy. It's dumb because it produces powerfully negative financial outcomes.

In later chapters, you will be presented with a vast array of data that in no uncertain terms document the connection between how employees are treated, how they in turn perform, and how that in turn affects the company's financial performance. The sheer volume of evidence is overwhelming and indisputable. In the meantime, consider this thumbnail statement.

When people are perceived as a cost and not a resource, when they are treated as a liability and not an asset, when no one seems to know or care that they are there, they don't work well, and they don't stay.

That bears repeating: They don't work well. And they don't stay.

- In one recent Gallup survey, 17 percent of those interviewed were actively disengaged and were trying to subvert the organization in which they worked.[5] Fifty-four percent were passively disengaged; their bodies were still in the office but they had essentially left. Fifty percent were ready to change jobs.

No organization can flourish when half of its employees want to leave and almost three-fourths do not feel committed to the organization or engaged in the work it does.

- A growing number of people, especially those in their twenties and thirties, are leaving the fast track because work demands keep rising while satisfaction and payoffs continue to decline.

In 2005, Next Generation Consulting reported the results of its study on work trends.[6] They found that people who create and use knowledge, especially younger knowledge workers, were eager to reinvent their work experience so they could feel fulfilled. Within a balanced life, they wanted to work hard at work that was meaningful to them. In contrast, they found, the actual experiences of many knowledge workers are leaving them burnt out and frustrated.

For example, Spherion Corporation, a major supplier of part-time employees and outsourced workforce management to many global corporations, has been conducting research on the values and motives of employees for more than six years. Its most current data find the level of employee discontent is so great that the United States could incur more than $600 billion in workforce costs because of turnover in the next three to five years.[7]

With the breakdown of any implicit or actual contract based on mutual benefits and responsibilities between employees and organizations, increasing numbers of employees, especially women, are switching to the nonprofit sector, are striking out on their own, or leaving work altogether.

Organized labor stands to benefit from this growing dissatisfaction. The litany of losses is familiar: massive layoffs, sending work offshore, slow growth in wages, and reduced benefits in health care and pensions. When unions use these losses as a rallying cry for the workforce to mobilize and join up, many people will find that appealing. A stronger labor movement has huge political implications. With the help of sophisticated technology, organized labor's political machine has been able to get millions of union members, who usually vote Democratic, to the polls in recent elections.

A Psychological Recession is not just an idea; it is a real phenomenon with real consequences, all of them bad. When people are scared and depressed for a long time, despair and fear replace confidence and optimism. Try running a company with workers who feel like that. In the larger economic picture, it is really dangerous that a Psychological Recession characterizes most people's views and moods when two-thirds of our gross domestic product is based on consumer spending, which is profoundly affected by consumer confidence.

> A Psychological Recession is not just an idea; it is a real phenomenon with real consequences, all of them bad.

The widespread Psychological Recession is largely the result of organizations no longer responding to employees as key assets. There can be no question that this has led to too many scared, alienated, and uninvolved employees. Feeling as if you're being endlessly pushed from here to nowhere and no one cares is not an ideal condition for individuals, their organizations, or the nation. The headless horseman is not a good role model; we need leaders who really believe it when they say that people are the most important asset.

CHAPTER THREE

FEELINGS MATTER— "SOFT" IS "HARD"

A FEW YEARS AGO I was at a meeting of a board I'd been on for eleven years. The board was responsible for two financial companies, a regional bank and an auto finance company. The detailed discussions about quantitative outcomes, especially financial ones, had gone on for hours and my mind started wandering. *We never talk about the people part of the equation,* I thought, and that's the part that really interests me.

In that second I realized two things: one, upper management is only interested in results, and the language it uses is quantitative; and two, in most organizations employees no longer count as stakeholders. Even though you'll hear the decisionmakers say, repeatedly and in earnest tones, "People are our most important asset," the truth is that few senior executives are eager to hear about employee issues. They are also essentially uninterested in the part of the organization that's identified with those issues, the Human Resources department. Basically, they are largely uninterested in their employees.

Until roughly fifteen years ago, Human Resource departments justified their activities by citing increased employee morale, satisfaction, and happiness. Human Resources thus spoke to executives in its own language, which was not the one used by executives. As a direct result of the difference in priorities—or the gap in language—HR managers could not mount an effective case for their contributions and could not earn the respect of the people who controlled the organization's decisions and resources.

Today, there is an enormous body of evidence that the "soft" variables that HR tends to deal with have hard outcomes —quantifiable, measurable outcomes—and it is time for senior management to pay attention.

Much of what we have long thought was true about organizational dynamics is not true. In August 2002, James Clifton, chairman and CEO of the Gallup organization, challenged many widespread assumptions about work and workers. Calling on the responses that Gallup has accumulated and analyzed from millions of people about what they truly believe and want, Clifton showed that much of what was taken for granted is in fact incorrect.[1]

> The "soft" variables that HR tends to deal with have hard outcomes—quantifiable, measurable outcomes.

- The premise is that CEOs care about people because they often say, *People are our most important asset.*
  The fact is that CEOs don't care about the people; they care about results.
- The premise is that Americans ground their identities in their family and community.
  The fact is that since the early 1990s most people identify themselves in terms of their jobs, their job titles, and the brand image of their employers.

- The premise is that employees in the United States are fully involved in their work.
  The fact is that only 25 percent have a strong commitment to their job.
- The premise is that employees are really motivated by compensation and benefits.
  The fact is that an employee's manager is the key to that person being fully involved.
- The premise is that the majority of managers are effective.
  The fact is that far fewer than one in four are strong and caring and therefore effective.
- The premise is that our economy is stronger than ever because we have visionary CEOs.
  The fact is that *most* CEOs are cost cutters, and cost cutters are never great executives.

Clifton argues that what is really needed now are people who understand the critical importance of "intangibles" because it is the intangibles, not tangible assets like capital or physical facilities, that create value through initiative and innovation.

A major intangible is the spirit of an organization. It is dramatically clear that, in too many of our organizations, the spirit is broken. The defensive focus on cost cutting has created a malaise that permeates all areas of the organization and squashes any optimistic sense of profit building. Recovering from that malaise starts with a reinvigorated investment in the "people" aspects.

HEART TRUMPS HEAD

It's not hard to understand why so many executive were not interested in the issues involved in managing people. It's because these executives themselves were judged primarily in terms of quarterly financial reports and the company's stock price. The link between financial outcomes and the effective management of people was not immediately obvious.

Then, in 1988, came a major breakthrough. The Sears organization commissioned a study of the causal links between employees' attitudes, customer responses, and financial outcomes.[2] This seminal study concluded that employees who enjoyed working at Sears earned higher ratings from customers on the service they delivered and that more satisfied customers led to higher profits.

Rucci, Kirn, and Quinn, the authors of the study, found that every five percent improvement in the employees' sense of satisfaction (today we call it commitment and engagement) led to a 1.3 percent rise in the customers' level of satisfaction, which in turn produced a 0.5 percent increase in the store's revenues. For the first time a study linked employee and customer *feelings* with their *behavior* and an explicit financial result.

Today, literally hundreds of studies link human emotions with quantitative outcomes, particularly financial ones. Almost every day we learn of new data supporting the view that failure to really manage employees—to capture their hearts as well as their minds—is dangerous to the financial health of an organization. The accumulated evidence is simply overwhelming.

While academics argue the validity of different causal models, the take-home message is very clear: feelings matter, and they matter a lot. If employees believe they are being treated fairly, there's a better chance the organization will succeed. But if people are convinced they're being taken for granted or treated as anonymous, faceless and interchangeable widgets, the odds of financial success are low.

> It's all about emotions. Feelings always win out over facts, because how people *feel* determines how they *act*.

It's all about emotions. Feelings always win out over facts, because how people *feel* determines how they *act*. When people feel they're treated well, when they're respected and trusted and much is expected of them, they voluntarily work better and harder. The reverse is also true.

Negative feelings usually lead to negative results. I can attest to this from my own experience. When I was an undergraduate, I worked one summer as a clerk in the headquarters of the Gossard Corset Company in Manhattan. My job involved typing up shipping orders—an original and five copies of each. It was excruciatingly boring. In those days, making copies required thin onionskin paper and carbon paper. To get the required number of copies I had to slip a piece of carbon paper between each of five pieces of onionskin paper. Then I tapped the papers this way and that so they lined up. Next, I inserted them in the roller of my big manual typewriter. I would then use my index and middle fingers to type the shipping information. I was so underemployed that I daydreamed all day.

But there was something else to think about. The office boss was a martinet, a stickler for observing rules at their literal worst, including keeping track of how many minutes we spent going to the bathroom. She was a micromanager, furiously picky about everything and arrogantly certain no one would do their job properly without her constant surveillance. Of course everything boomeranged. Because we weren't trusted we didn't trust her, and we wanted her to fail. Because she was the most interesting thing in the office, we thought about her a lot; because we wanted her to fail, we spent a lot of time figuring out sneaky ways to sabotage our work. We succeeded so well that she was demoted and one of the clerks was appointed office manager over her head.

Bad management persists to this day, with the same negative results. In May 2003 Judy Rosen, then CEO of the consulting group Concours, told a group of us about her miserable trip trying to fly to a meeting in Houston.

"The weather was terrible," she said, "and flights were being cancelled or delayed left and right. Most of us were flying for business and so we *had* to get to our destinations and as close to on time as possible. Time was dragging on and we were getting pretty damn angry because we didn't know what was going on and no one was helping us.

"About twenty of us ended up standing in front of the ticket counter, where we were thoroughly ignored. Finally the ticket agent glanced in our direction and said, 'I don't care about you [customers] since my management doesn't care about me.'"

Given half a chance, none of those twenty customers will ever fly on that airline again.

This is not nuclear physics. It's pretty easy to create a positive atmosphere, and pretty easy to see that a positive atmosphere increases the chance of success. That's especially obvious in organizations that largely depend on excellent service. For one thing, treating employees fairly and well typically results in lower turnover and reduced training costs. But the most significant outcome of respecting and valuing employees is a level of extraordinary customer service, and that is a major competitive advantage.

> The most significant outcome of respecting and valuing employees is a level of extraordinary customer service, and that is a major competitive advantage.

Starbucks Corporation, for example, is well known for its positive treatment of even low-level employees.[3] Anyone who works at least 20 hours a week is eligible for health insurance and a stock option grant. Starbucks' turnover is near the bottom of the range for its industry, its service levels are high despite the repetitiveness of many of its jobs, and since the IPO in June 1992, Starbucks shares have risen by 3,500 percent.

Another example occurred when the executives of the Four Seasons Hotels realized they could not deliver outstanding customer service unless their employees really took the well-being of every guest to heart.[4] That's what the hotels teach, and it's what guides the behavior of every one of their employees. In a Four Seasons hotel, new guests find themselves in the pleasantest of conversations with the bellman, the receptionist, or anyone else they happen to meet.

The results are impressive. The Four Seasons Hotels worldwide have one of the lowest employee turnover rates in the hospitality industry. *Fortune* has named the Four Seasons as one of the "100 Best Companies to Work For" every year, including 2006. The stock multiple is nearly double that of its closest peer. It's really true: "soft" feelings have hard outcomes.

PEOPLE ARE NOT COMMODITIES

The key idea is very old but somehow it has to be continuously rediscovered: People are smart, especially when it comes to things that directly affect them, and they know what is going on. Most of the time you can fool only a few of the people, and even then not for long.

When organizations treat employees as commodities and stop making commitments to them, employees reciprocate. They cease being involved in the organization's work, and they are no longer committed to the organization's success. They simply stop caring.

This is a major reason why massive downsizing is risky, even though it may seem a good idea from the perspective of top management. Because labor is one of the largest expenses in any undertaking, downsizing is very appealing to executives, especially those in technical or service industries desperate to swiftly improve their balance sheets.[5]

But the evidence does not support the idea that cutting people results in an immediate improvement in profits. The American Management Association's survey of companies that had reduced payrolls reported that only 45 percent had profited from that action within a year and, hardly surprising, one-third of those companies reported a decline in employee morale.[6]

Near the end of the twentieth century, massive cutting of the bloated costs of organizations with entitlement cultures made sense. But wholesale downsizing of reasonably healthy organizations in the first decade of the twenty-first century probably did far more harm than good. The psychological fall-out is very, very expensive.

Using large layoffs as the first tool of economic defense when times grow hard tells employees they are expendable. Massive layoffs usually produce mistrust, anxiety, and anger, and these are hardly the ideal mental states for productivity, creativity, and collaboration.

Organizations need to rethink their response to tough economic times. Careful consideration and judicious action are called for. Organizations will fare best when cutting costs through layoffs occurs only after all other alternatives have been tried.[7]

Actually, it is often the case that costs *rise* after layoffs. The organization loses skilled workers, who are expensive to replace, and there is greater turnover and absenteeism, more sick days, lower productivity, and less creativity. There is also a greater chance of stronger unions and strikes.

COMMITMENT IS NOT KINDNESS

Unless an organization has communicated the reasons for draconian cost cutting in a very persuasive way, when organizations decide to cut costs through huge layoffs, the result is very predictable and very negative: an angry, alienated, fearful, or uncommitted labor force. In the global competitive economy, no organization can afford that. When times are hard, employees need more commitment from their organizations—not less. A greater commitment to employees is not "kindness"; it is an investment with a great rate of return, and it is at the heart of an organization's ability to succeed beyond the short term.

Too many people today are too fearful. People who are afraid tend to work as hard as necessary to keep their jobs but contribute as little intellectual capital and discretionary effort as possible.[8] Discretionary effort is the amount of effort or energy that people contribute beyond what is needed to keep their jobs. Intellectual capital is the accumulation of people's experience, skills, knowledge and ideas that they could contribute if they were willing to.

In the brutal, unending competition of a global economy, the idea that an organization that commits to its employees will be better off in the long run can seem pretty laughable, rather like Don Quixote attacking windmills. But the departure of serious talent isn't smart, even in the short term. In a Darwinian economy the competition only increases, in bad times as well as good, and high-potential people are the key resource. The cost of lost knowledge, leadership, and creativity will always be too high.

At a time when reducing labor costs is foremost in executives' minds, it is easy to forget that cutting costs as a key strategy often only delays death.

Organizations have a far better chance of succeeding when their people are committed, energized, and engaged instead of fearful, exhausted, and overwhelmed. When people feel they are valued and they can earn some security, they are much more likely to make a commitment to the organization, take on greater responsibilities, and initiate positive changes.

Arguably, leadership's most important task now is to reinstate employees as stakeholders and increase the organization's commitment to them. It is very much in the organization's best interest to do so.

CHAPTER FOUR

BAD MANAGEMENT IS (REALLY) EXPENSIVE

THIS CHAPTER IS ABOUT NUMBERS—numbers that speak largely to failure.

Failure or success can be measured in many different ways. For example, is there a high level of energy and innovation, or do large numbers of people come to work only to read the paper, gossip, and complain? This chapter measures failure in terms of emotions. How do people *feel* about their jobs (mostly negative, it turns out) and how are they likely to *act* when they feel (as most do) that they're being treated badly?

What most executives fail to recognize is the link between feelings (both employees and customers) and the organization's bottom line. In this chapter, I've elected to make the case for the importance of feelings in terms of financial results because that is what matters most to executive decision makers.

Many organizations—probably most—operate as if they don't know about the costs of bad management. It should be obvious—but often is not—that alienated employees result in low productivity, poor retention, and high absenteeism. There is a mountain of data screaming for attention, data that verify, over and over, the financial outcome of employees' emotions. Up to now, most senior executives have been largely unaware of these data. It's wakeup time.

The following are but a small sample from the body of many recent large-scale studies; together, they constitute a powerful warning.

MANY EMPLOYEES FEEL NEGATIVELY ABOUT WORK

In January 2003, the Human Resources consulting firm Towers Perrin released the results of its study titled "Working Today: Exploring Employees' Emotional Connection to Their Jobs."[1] The study asked 1100 people from 1004 companies with 500 or more employees to describe how they felt at work.

- Fifty-five percent responded with terms like "exhausted, confused, and unsupported."
- One-third said they felt extremely negative. The most common complaints included boredom because the work was not challenging, heavy workloads, and feelings of helplessness. People felt the work they did, their skills, and they themselves weren't important to their organizations.

No wonder 28 percent of those who felt negatively were actively looking for a new job. The rest had already quit even though they continued to show up for work each day.

The Towers Perrin study found a "statistically significant correlation" between how employees felt about work and shareholder return over the five years from 1998 to 2002. The more positively employees felt, the higher the companies' profits and share price.

The Number of Unhappy Employees Continues to Increase

The Conference Board hired TNS, a market research firm, to interview people about their attitudes toward work in a sample of 5000 households. The results were reported in March 2005.[2] The percent of employees who were happy with their jobs had dropped from 59 percent ten years earlier to 50 percent.

The decline was found among people doing all kinds of work, but the largest drop was among people aged 35 to 44 who were earning $25,000 to $35,000 a year. This may bring about a serious challenge to employers because the retiring boomers will be replaced by Generation X and Generation Y, many of whose members reject the idea that work should be the determining factor in how they live their lives.

Many Employees Feel Resentful

In 2002, the international consulting company AON Limited reported a large number of employees in the United Kingdom were anxious, stressed, and resentful because of pressure to increase performance without any increase in rewards.[3] In a study involving 1,800 workers, AON reported declining commitment for the third year in a row in every age group, income group, job classification, and industry. While nearly 80 percent believed their organization would be fine, only 55 percent believed they would benefit from the success of the organization. Appropriately, only 40 percent believed their employer deserved any loyalty.

Low Rates of Employee Commitment and Loyalty Are Very Expensive

The one-third of employees who are alienated from their companies will actively seek a new job within two years, and 50 percent will find a new employer within five.

Replacing clerical and shop workers costs, on average, 50 percent of their salary. The figure for executives is 200 percent of their base salary.

The Washington, DC-based Corporate Advisory Board estimates the cost of replacing an expert in information technology as 1.75 times that person's salary. Replacing a front-line staff person who delivers good customer service will take almost half of their annual pay. Organizations with very high turnover, like call centers, are bleeding money.

Downsizing Leads to Resentment, Which Leads to Terrible Customer Service

Employee resentment in combination with employee downsizing is very likely to prove extraordinarily expensive; the combination practically guarantees terrible service. Even some highly admired companies, like Home Depot and Dell, have managed to alienate their customers as a direct result of their cost cutting.[4]

Customer service at Home Depot became a lesser priority than it had been. As a result, Home Depot's sales increased one percent in the first quarter of 2006 while sales at customer-friendly Lowe's, its main competitor, increased by 5.7 percent.

Dell depends directly on customer sales through the phone and the Internet. But some of their call centers have fewer than 500 employees. Recently, it was not unusual for customers to be put on hold for 30 minutes before they reached a human being *to place an order* or to solve a problem. In 2005, Dell removed the toll-free phone number for service from its Web site in an effort to discourage calls. The number was put back in the spring of 2006.

Northwest Airlines is bankrupt. To save costs, the company removed pillows and stopped giving out small bags of pretzels at the same time that it raised fares and cut the number of flights. Northwest is the number-one airline in customer dissatisfaction and, since management pressured pilots and other employees into deep pay cuts, they are probably number one in employee dissatisfaction. Major customer and employee dissatisfaction is not a strategy that can produce profits.

Many Employees Want to Move to a New Job

In the United States the Web portal Yahoo conducted an online poll of about 2,600 workers in 2004. Employees reported feeling overworked and underappreciated; many were resentful of the lack of an increase in pay.[5] But with an expanding job market, unhappy employees are also feeling more empowered and optimistic. Almost half of those interviewed were already seeking a new job or planned to do so within the year.

Another study conducted by Spherion Employment Solutions reported that 52 percent of employees wanted to move to a new job, and 75 percent said they wanted to do that within the year.[6]

Unhappy Employees Are Unproductive Employees

Studies by The Corporate Leadership Council and the Society for Human Resource Management reveal clear connections between productivity and employees' views and feelings.[7] Their data showed that:

1. Sixty-five percent of employees will change jobs when the economy is strong.
2. A full three-fourths of employees, 76 percent, said their commitment was up for grabs.
3. Seventy-one percent of HR professionals are concerned about the loss of employee involvement, and 61 percent are increasingly worried about productivity.
4. Eighty-eight percent of HR professionals are concerned about their organization's relentless pressure on employees to do more with less.

Like Employee Loyalty, Customer Loyalty Cannot Be Taken for Granted

Gallup has found that only about 21 percent of an organization's customers are fully engaged and a like percent are engaged, for a total of 42 percent.[8] That's not good. It means that more than half of customers are *not* engaged: 30 percent are nonengaged and almost the same number actively disengaged, for a total of almost 60 percent. No organization can ever forget it is in a competitive battle for the employees and customers it really wants to keep.

THE GALLUP SURVEYS OF ENGAGEMENT

Since 1992, the Gallup organization has used its well-respected Employment Engagement Survey, known as the Gallup Q12, to assess an organization's culture and its effect on staff perform-ance as measured in terms of employee feelings and attitudes. The questions that correlate most strongly with business success or failure involve people knowing what they should do, having the tools and skills and opportunity to do what they do best, and having a supervisor who recognizes their contribution, supports their development, and cares about them as a people.[9]

Based on millions of responses to the Q12 assessment, Gallup believes this instrument can measure the status of all kinds of businesses. More significantly, the high correlation with levels of customer commitment, staff turnover, productivity, safety and profitability makes it a *predictive* instrument as well.[10]

The most important financial results that the Q12 reveals have to do with turnover and related costs. Here is just one very telling statistic. In 2001, Gallup estimated that a call center with 150 employees and 40 percent turnover would find it cost £200,000 (approximately $392,340) a year to replace those work-ers.[11] In 2002, Gallup examined the expense created by absen-teeism. It cost business in the United Kingdom £11 billion a year (approximately $21 billion) for days taken ostensibly for ill-ness.[12] These are huge costs that beg for remedial action.

Gallup finds employee discontent wherever workers feel that

- Managers don't care about them as individuals.
- Managers don't respect them enough to hear their input .

- Managers focus on their weaknesses and not their strengths.
- They don't know what managers expect from them.
- Their jobs don't make use of their talents.

Gallup collected a database of 4.5 million employees in 12 industries in the three years from 2002 to 2005 and reports consistently low levels of employee involvement.[13] While the specific percentages vary in Gallup's many studies because of differences among samples, years, or countries, the basic numbers are 20/60/20; 20 percent of employees are engaged, 60 percent are not engaged and 20 percent are actively disengaged. That is a stunning finding. Approximately four-fifths of employees are either actively disengaged or simply not engaged.[14]

Similar numbers have been reported by the Corporate Leadership Council, Towers Perrin, and other well-respected research-consulting firms.[15] A 2005 Towers Perrin *Global Workforce Survey* reported the results from 85,000 full-time employees worldwide in large and mid-sized firms. In this study, only 14 percent of the worldwide sample were highly engaged in their work; 62 percent were not engaged or moderately engaged at best; and 24 percent were described as actively disengaged.[16]

The problem is not restricted to U.S. companies. In a study of British employees, Gallup reported engaged employees were 19 percent of the labor force; nonengaged were 61 percent; and 20 percent were disengaged.[17] This means that the great major-

To say this another way:

- An astonishing 80 percent of employees do not care about their organization or their work.
- In the majority of organizations, about 60 percent of employees work only enough to keep their jobs and another 20 percent would hurt the organization if they could.

ity of employees, more than 80 percent, are not committed to their jobs or their organizations. Gallup believes that the actively disengaged employees, those who are often blatantly negative, cost the British economy between £37.2 and 38.9 billion ($64.8 to 66.1 billion) because of high turnover, low retention rates, high absenteeism and low performance or productivity levels.

Recent Gallup results in the United States found some improvement, but the numbers are still discouraging. Twenty-nine percent of employees are actively engaged in their work, 54 percent are not engaged, and 17 percent are actively disengaged.[18] This means less than one-third of employees are energized and excited by their work and their organization; slightly more than half are walking through the day just putting in time; and 17 percent are dis-seminating their unhappiness in an effort to undermine their colleagues' commitment to the organization.

> Twenty-nine percent of employees are actively engaged in their work, 54 percent are not engaged, and 17 percent are actively disengaged.

This last group, the people who are actively disengaged, represent a particular danger. I call them "boils" because they are centers of infection; they spread disengagement and hostility among employees. Alarmingly, the percent of employees who are "not engaged" or who are "actively disengaged" increases the longer an employee has been with that company. When people join a company they are emotionally primed to become a part of the organization. Their disenchantment, or disengagement, usually starts within the first six months of their employment.[19]

ENGAGEMENT AND PRODUCTIVITY: THE NEW CENTURY EXAMPLE

New Century, a specialty mortgage lender, used Gallup's Q12 instrument in October 2001 to learn whether engaged account executives were more productive than nonengaged employees, and, if so, by how much.[20] After the first assessment, productivity was tracked for six months. The results were very revealing. Nonengaged account executives produced 23 percent less revenue, and actively disengaged employees produced 28 percent less revenue than engaged account executives.

In light of these results, New Century created and set in motion actions to improve employee engagement, and then conducted two followup Q12s to assess changes. What they learned is instructive: Engagement *leads* to better performance rather than simply correlates with it.

When, for example, New Century retail branches that had successfully improved their Q12 scores twice in a row were compared with branches whose scores were flat or declined twice in a row, the per-person growth in revenue in the branches with improved engagement scores was six times higher than those where the engagement score had not improved. These results held true irrespective of the initial Q12 score. Over one year, the changes in per-person revenue were:

Q12 scores declined	1.8 percent
Q12 scores inconsistent	5.4 percent
Consistent improvement	12.1 percent

WHAT ALL THESE DATA MEAN

Organizations are paying a lot for really bad management practices.

It's past time for organizations to get the connection. Management practices that make employees feel insignificant and of little value bring predictable results, including lost productivity, an increase in avoidable accidents, high turnover, absenteeism, and low levels of commitment to the organization and its customers.

Management practices that alienate people produce employees who don't care. Employees who are alienated have no interest in working hard, much less in being creative and inno-vative. Employees who are alienated produce customers who are alienated.

The data support the powerful conclusion that alienating employees and customers is a certain route to failure and red ink.

CHAPTER FIVE

GOOD MANAGEMENT (REALLY) MAKES MONEY

I F BAD MANAGEMENT PRODUCES negative results, as is indisputably reflected in dollars and cents on the bottom line (see Chapter 4), does good management produce positives? Absolutely.

Organizations that really value and involve their employees have higher levels of growth, market value, return on assets, and returns to shareholders. That is not wishful thinking; that is the inescapable conclusion of the data from hundreds of quantified studies. The goal of this chapter is to present that data in such a way that corporate decision makers freely embrace it.

The positive quantitative outcomes presented in this chapter are largely the result of management's support and respect for employees. These organizations operate from a deep belief that the essential competitive edge lies in excellent employees. To achieve highly successful, productive organizations, executive decision makers must believe, *really* believe, that people are the vital asset so they are willing to make long-term investments of large amounts of time and some amount of money in them. That core value must cascade through all levels of management.

It's all about management style. In these cultures, bosses direct and order infrequently; most of the time managers and executives teach, inspire, listen, and act. These results-driven organizations are supportive of employees because they know that in very real terms it pays off. They know that there is a direct relationship between how employees perform and the organization's success or failure.

In particular, the relationships people have with their bosses are critical in determining whether they invest in or separate from an organization and the work it does. (For more on nurturing this relationship, see Chapter 7.) Managers who alienate subordinates need to be replaced by people who are interpersonally adept.

> The relationships people have with their bosses are critical in determining whether they invest in or separate from an organization and the work it does.

Management must also realize that how people *feel* is generally more important than what people *think;* emotions are significantly more influential than reason in creating attitudes and influencing choices. And lastly, what counts in creating the positive outcomes is not a single, one-way action but layers of dynamic interaction—employees with other employees, employees with management, and employees with customers. Especially the customers.

IT'S THE INTERACTION BETWEEN EMPLOYEES AND CUSTOMERS

Success or failure is determined by the extent to which individual employees are involved with the organization and how those feelings lead them to interact with customers. Of course, customers can also have emotional connections to the company; that's what brand loyalty is all about. But the key element, and the one that managers can directly influence, is employee engagement. That is the source of behaviors that are either profitable or costly because they color the quality of interactions with customers. Employees who are strongly engaged with their organization are better able to emotionally involve a customer and create strong connections with that customer. And that is what creates high levels of customer retention, profits, and growth.

Customers do not have interactions with an abstraction like an organization. They have interactions with people, one on one, employees who are pleasant and helpful—or the opposite. And all too often customers deal not with any human being at all but with a machine offering telephone-tree choices, which guarantees customer frustration. All these interactions, both positive and negative, are very powerful in terms of creating an enduring relationship with customers or killing whatever relationship previously existed.

> Customers do not have interactions with an abstraction like an organization. They have interactions with people, one on one.

These views are brilliantly supported by Gallup organization members John Fleming, Curt Coffman, and James Harter in an outstanding article in the *Harvard Business Review*.[1] Fleming, Coffman, and Harter set out to create a Human Sigma, a measure of human performance which, like Six Sigma, would reduce variability and improve performance. Their approach rested on several assumptions:

- Emotions are a greater influence on the judgment of employees and customers than reason.
- The nature of employee–customer interactions has to be measured locally because variability within an organization is extensive.

- The local manager has an enormous impact on whether employees are emotionally committed or not.
- It is possible to develop and use a single measure of the effectiveness of the customer–employee encounter, and that measure will correlate strongly with financial outcomes.

After years of experience with hundreds of companies, they tested, refined, and cross-validated their results in almost 2000 business units in ten companies. All ten used best practices for improving the employee–customer interaction, and all ten had impressive results. In 2003 they outperformed their five largest peers by 26 percent in gross margins and by 85 percent in sales growth.

The Gallup researchers learned that the "extremely satisfied" customers consisted of two very different groups, one made up of people with strong emotional connections to the company and another group without those feelings, whose satisfaction was rational rather than emotional. The first group contributed far more financially than the second. Actually, the behaviors of the rationally satisfied customers were the same as customers who were dissatisfied.

Reinforcing this finding is the recent report by the international consulting group Towers Perrin. Its researchers found that engaged employees display two important traits: they think about their work, and they are very focused on the customer. The Towers Perrin report documents the financial impact. Companies with engaged employees tend to exceed their industry's annual average growth in revenue by at least one percentage point.[2] In contrast, companies in which most employees are either not engaged or are actively disengaged report their average annual growth fell below the industry average by one or two percent.

Measuring emotional involvement, both negative and positive, of *both* employees and customers is a much more valid predictor of financial and operational performance than assessments of either customers or employees alone. And measurements of individual employees and small business units are more telling than measures of an organization because there is an immense amount of variability and averages hide critical data.

Vivaldi, a New York brand strategy firm, reported in its 2002 Brand Leadership Study that when customers gave a brand a high rating, that brand outperformed the market by a factor of 1.6.[3] But when *both* employees and customers ranked the brand highly, that brand outperformed the market by 3.2 times. In five-year returns to shareholders, the Vivaldi study found:

The S&P Index	100
Companies receiving high ratings from consumers	160
Companies receiving high ratings from *both* consumers and employees	320

All three of these studies (Gallup, Towers Perrin, and Vivaldi) offer powerful evidence about the interaction between employees and customers, but that is not the only evidence. There are hundreds of studies that correlate independently assessed employee feelings and business results, and they all support the view that sustained profitability depends largely on the enthusiasm generated by the customer's experience, which, in turn, depends largely on the enthusiasm and involvement of the employee serving the customer. In quantitative terms, 70 percent of how the customer perceives your brand (or your organization) is the result of the customer's experience with your employees.[4]

Fully involved customers are worth their weight in platinum. They deliver a 23 percent financial premium over the average customer. Business units that are in the top quartile of customer involvement outperform all other units financially by a factor of two:one.[5]

GOOD MANAGEMENT
IS PROFITABLE

What happens when organizations use the most effective management practices and weave them seamlessly into the organization's culture? All kinds of positive, measurable results:

- Higher revenues
- Higher ROI
- Higher profits
- Higher earnings per share
- Higher share price
- Increased productivity
- Lower turnover costs among both customers and employees

These forward-thinking companies typically outperform their competitors in product quality, customer service, and effective innovation. The proof is in the data, of which the following is just a small sampling.

Motivated Employees and Profitablity

In 2002, the global consulting firm Watson Wyatt published the Human Capital Index (HCI), one of the first attempts to quantify the relationship between how an organization relates to its people and how those practices relate to financial results.[6] Like the three Gallup researchers, Fleming, Coffman, and Harter,[7] Watson Wyatt found that superior employee and management practices are a leading—rather than a lagging—indicator of how well an organization will do financially.[8]

For its study, Watson Wyatt compiled three years' worth of data from 405 companies with an average of 9,000 employees and $1.5 billion in annual revenue, and then used that data to construct each company's HCI.[9] Then, comparing HCIs to shareholder returns over three years, Watson Wyatt found that:

- Companies with an HCI above 75 had an average annual return of 70 percent.
- Companies with an HCI between 25 and 75 averaged an annual return of 12 percent.
- Companies with an HCI lower than 25 brought their investors an average *loss* of 6 percent.

In 1999 and 2001, Watson Wyatt administered HCI surveys to 51 organizations in the United States and Europe. Using five-year total returns to shareholders, the data revealed that:

- Organizations with low HCI scores averaged a 21 percent total return.
- Organizations with medium scores averaged 39 percent.
- Those with high HCI scores averaged 64 percent.

Researchers at the Institute for Employment Studies reported similar profitability in a major British retail chain.[10] They found that when employees were satisfied with line management and the company's values, they were proud of their work, loyal, and felt a sense of ownership. A one-point increase in employee satisfaction resulted in an increase of up to £200,000 (approximately $394,000) in sales per month in a store. That's an annual increase of £1,200,000 or $2,363,000 in the chain.

Costco versus Wal-Mart's Sam's Club

Costco is much more generous to employees than is Wal-Mart's Sam's Club.[11] At Costco, 82 percent of employees receive an average of $5,735 in health insurance annually compared with 47 percent of Sam's Club workers, who average $3,500. Ninety-one percent of Costco's employees are in line for a pension compared to 64 percent of Sam's Club. And while the average hourly wage at Sam's Club is $11.52, at Costco it is $15.97. The cost of not being generous is very high. Sam's Club's cost of labor and overhead is almost double that of Costco (17 percent of sales compared with nine percent), and labor turnover at Sam's Club during the first year on the job is a very expensive 21 percent compared with Costco's six percent. And Costco's sales are about double that of Sam's Club despite a smaller number of stores.[12]

Wall Street has historically valued Wal-Mart's Sam's Club business strategy more than Costco's. But Costco's strategy of greater commitments to employees results in a much higher sales-per-employee ratio—102,000 Sam's Club employees generated $35 billion in sales in 2004 compared with Costco's $34 billion with one-third fewer employees. Costco's model of far more generous wages and benefits results in much higher levels of retaining customers and employees and much lower labor and overhead costs. Costco's strategy of greater commitment to employees has generated lower costs and greater profits—$13,647 versus $11,039 in operating profit per hourly employee.

SAS Institute

SAS is a privately held software company with an extremely supportive, employee-friendly culture.[13] In an April 2003 interview on the CBS program "Sixty Minutes," CEO James Goodnight emphasized the value of employees. He remarked that 95 percent of his assets walk out the door every night, and his job is to get them to return.

SAS has on-site health care and day care and numerous programs that support work–life issues. Most employees are on flexible schedules and work either four or five days a week. They receive as much time off as they need to deal with illness in the family or elder care. Particularly interesting is the company's view that an imbalance in people's work–life commitments is the result of jobs being poorly designed, with inadequate planning and prioritizing.

Goodnight was very clear that he viewed every Human Resource program that responded to employees' needs as a positive investment with a marvelous return in growth, retention, and profits. Clearly, that investment pays off. In 2002, SAS had achieved 26 years of double-digit growth.

The turnover rate in 2002 in the software industry was 28 percent; SAS's was four percent, and in 2003 it was running at three percent. Goodnight estimates the low turnover rate saves $60–80 million a year in replacement costs. He also believes it is the key to SAS's customer retention: a phenomenal 98 percent.

BEST COMPANIES TO WORK FOR

Best Employers—large or small, publicly or privately held, in a very wide range of industries—generate more value in terms of revenue, profit growth, return on assets, and share price than other companies do, and they share their success to a far greater extent with their employees and their communities.

A great place to work results in very high levels of satisfied employees and trust in management, and that shows up in the bottom line.[14] These companies provide plenty of hard data supporting the basic premise that organizations that really value and involve their employees do better financially. Here, too, the volume of research data is so large that I have selected a representative sample.

Start with one dimension that everyone recognizes as critical: return to shareholders. If the same amount of money had been invested from 1998 through 2002 in the S&P 500, the Russell 3000, and The 100 Best Companies to Work For, investors would have achieved an annual return of:

- –0.71 percent for the S&P 500
- –0.56 percent for the Russell 3000
- +9.86 percent for the 100 Best

The results are similar for the *Fortune* Survey of Most Admired Companies: Over five years, from 1999 to 2004, shareholder returns for companies identified as America's most admired averaged 26 percent, two-and-a-half times the return from peer comparison companies.[15]

Vanderbilt University and Hewitt Associates, a worldwide Human Resources consulting firm, studied the companies on *Fortune's* 100 Best Companies to Work For from 1998 to 2003 and found that they outperformed similar organizations with cumulative stock returns that averaged 50 percent above the market norm.[16] The data showed that organizations with progressive Human Resources programs that addressed employees' significant needs had greater income and return on assets and spent more money on R&D.

The trend continues. The publicly traded companies on *Fortune's* 2007 list of 100 Best Companies to Work For consistently beat the market over the preceding 10 years.[17]

Over the decade from 1998 to 2007, these companies achieved an average annual return of 18.9 percent, which was more than double the 8.4 percent return of the S&P 500.[17]

Best Employers are not limited to the United States. In 2003, Hewitt and Associates created a list of Best Employers in Australia and examined the comparative financial data from 2000 to 2003. The Best Employers' revenue grew 13 percent, compared to seven percent at other companies.[18] The growth in profits was even more dramatic. Profits for Best Employers increased by 21 percent but *fell* 44 percent for other companies.

One reason Best Employers excel financially is lower turnover. Many studies by the HR consulting firm Hewitt have found that Best Employers around the world have much lower turnover costs—about 50 percent lower than the average in their industry—because their retention rates are significantly higher than other companies.[19] Best Companies to Work For also have much larger pools of talent to choose from because they average twice as many applications per job. Even when the job market is poor, the best talent chooses to join the best companies.

However, even Best Companies are not completely immune to the reality of layoffs. Almost half of them had layoffs in 2002. But rather than alienating their people, they handled the situation in such a way that employees still felt positively toward the company and people understood why layoffs had become necessary.[20]

Take the case of Xilinx, a semiconductor company that was number four in The Best Companies list in 2002. When it first became clear that it needed to lower costs, Xilinx cut salaries rather than people. The very first people affected were top management, who elected to cut their salaries by 20 percent. After that, employees were asked to accept cuts that averaged six percent.

Even though some layoffs did ultimately become necessary, Xilinx really delivered on a message of respect and consideration for employees, and employees responded by giving everything they had. With this kind of engagement, it's no accident that in the four-year period from 2002 to 2006, Xilinx's numbers improved dramatically:

- Revenues climbed from (in $M) $1,016.6 to $1,726.3.
- Gross margins rose from 45 percent to 62 percent.
- Profit margins soared from 5 percent to 21 percent.
- Diluted earnings per share went from $0.15 to $1.00.
- Stockholders' equity increased from $1,903.70 to $2,728.90.[21]

Best Companies to Work For are characterized by a real concern for people throughout the organization. This was apparent when 28,000 Australian employees were asked about their experiences and what they thought of their CEOs' philosophy and approach to managing people.[22] When the CEOs, in their turn, were asked to select the critical drivers of business success, their top four issues were people related, economic issues were number 10, and competitors their twelfth choice.

Studies of Best Employers find essentially the same characteristics in all of the companies who have earned that standing wherever they are in the world.

- Best Companies are run by people who simultaneously keep in mind the welfare of their people and their progress toward business goals.

- In these organizations, employees trust their bosses and have confidence in their abilities.
- Best Companies understand the importance of effective communication and know how to deliver it, so people feel they're heard and they're connected with the business.
- Best Companies make a serious investment in employees' careers; people know the organization's goals and what is expected of them.
- These organizations know what attracts, retains, and motivates employees. As a result, they don't permit aggressive and demeaning behaviors by bosses.
- In Best Companies, people believe they are in a meritocracy in which management really knows and appreciates what they contribute.

COMMITMENT CAN TAKE MANY FORMS

In the good old days, being committed to employees meant guaranteeing them a job for life. Clearly that is no longer an option (even the Japanese don't do it any more). But there are many other ways in which organizations can demonstrate their commitment to employees, and today's workers find them just as meaningful.

Here are just a few actions that companies can take to demonstrate commitment to employees. A much fuller discussion is in Chapter 8, which presents a broad range of possibilities, all centered on the notion that employees can earn the opportunity to choose the ones that are particularly valuable in their immediate lives.

Establish Family-Friendly Policies

Today's working parents and adult children with dependent parents are time deprived and multistressed. They want their employers to realize that work is only one of their responsibilities.

This affects the entire business world, for work–life conflict is painfully common: 85 percent of American workers have daily family responsibilities and one-third have children younger than 13 at home.[23] Increasingly, organizations that ignore employees' other commitments are seen as poor places to work; the best talent goes elsewhere.

In 2005, the consulting firm Work & Family Connection (now WFC Resources) announced the publication of *The Most Important Work–Life Related Studies,* a comprehensive summary of more than 250 academic and business reports and studies of corporate experiences from 1991 to 2003.[24] Susan Seitel, WFC president, observed that every kind of work–life support can be shown to have a positive financial impact. This includes child and elder care, financial and legal help, employee-assistance programs, parenting classes, training, and flexible work arrangements.

Flexible arrangements, flexible workplaces, flex hours, and compressed work weeks have become increasingly commonplace in the twenty-first century, and they have proved to be a boon for employees at all levels.[25] In an independently conducted study of 28 large American companies, with data from employee and customer surveys, flexibility proved to positively affect employee productivity, customer satisfaction, employee turnover, and cycle time. Not surprisingly, more satisfied employees—partly because of flexibility—were significantly more involved with their work, more likely to stay with their employer, and suffered less stress and burnout.

PNC Bank, a participant in the study, conducted a pilot program of a compressed work week. At the end of seven months, it found that

1. Exceptions in bond settlements fell by 50–75 percent.
2. Inquiries about bonds were answered the same day instead of a two-day turnaround.
3. Absenteeism dropped from 60 to nine days.
4. The reduced turnover of employees on a flexible program saved $112,750.

Another extremely common problem for working parents is access to affordable child care. Companies that can offer solutions have a major competitive advantage. Bright Horizons Family Solutions, a national company that provides quality child care, has found that companies that provide child care consistently outperform the S&P 500.[26]

One reason is that the majority of employers who provide child care—almost two-thirds in one study—have significantly reduced turnover.[27] As any employed parent of young children knows, a crisis is a kid who wakes up with a fever. Employers who provide backup child care reap an immediate financial benefit.[28] It has been estimated that for every $1 that organizations invest in child care, they will enjoy a $3 to $4 return in reduced turnover and sustained productivity.[29]

> It has been estimated that for every $1 that organizations invest in child care, they will enjoy a $3 to $4 return in reduced turnover and sustained productivity.

Put simply, family-friendly policies increase business success. People who are having difficulty because of work–life conflict are more than three times as likely to think of quitting (43 percent versus 14 percent). In contrast, employees in supportive environments with some flexibility and control over their work report greater satisfaction with their jobs and more commitment to helping their organization succeed. As a result, they generate measurable improvements in customer satisfaction and loyalty, revenues and profits, and shareholder value.[30]

Invest in Training

The studies of "visionary" companies by well-known author Jim Collins revealed that they outperformed other organizations on all financial measures.[31] In a comparison of 18 visionary organizations and 18 matched companies that were not visionary, the former had outperformed the American stock market by a factor of 15 and were six times more successful than the comparison organizations. How did they do it? Visionary companies invested heavily in the organization, specifically in R&D and facilities, in training and the professional development of staff, and in recruiting.

Financial analyst Mark Hulbert compared levels of corporate spending on training and development and analyzed how well the comparison companies did financially.[32] He found that the companies that spent the most on training (the top 20 percent) earned 16.2 percent on average in the years 1996 to 2001, compared to the Wilshire 500 average of 9.7 percent.

Communicate Honestly

People want and need to know, and smart leaders pay attention. The data about the effectiveness of communication reveal dramatic results. The Watson Wyatt 2004 WorkUSA study found that companies that opened the books and shared information with employees had a four times greater return to shareholders than companies that withheld information.[33]

In 2005, Watson Wyatt's Worldwide Study reported that effective communication:

1. Resulted in a 29.5 percent increase in share price.
2. Over five years resulted in shareholder returns that were nearly 50 percent greater than in organizations with less effective communication.
3. Resulted in significantly lower turnover rates: ($33.3 percent) than in industry peers with less effective communication (51.6 percent).[34]

Let Them Own a Piece of the Company

Effective communication is also important in employee stock ownership.[35] If organizations help employees realize that owning shares of stock means that they are truly owners of the company and their dedication is crucial for success, they will behave like owners. Then what happens is a companywide attitude of "we're going to do everything we can to make this business succeed!"

Act with Integrity

Five years of data reveal that organizations that practice corporate social responsibility enjoy the benefit of employees who contribute unstintingly because of their pride in being part of the organization. They also have very high retention rates.[36] Increasingly, customers and employees want the organizations they associate with to behave ethically and that is affecting employee and customer loyalty—and earnings.

WIDENING THE ROAD TO SUCCESS

Make no mistake, we still have a long way to go. Despite the gains that accrue from being a Best Employer, despite the (frankly obvious) practices that are needed to achieve this status, the majority of organizations still do not get it right.[37]

That is because most decision makers in the vast majority of organizations are convinced that people are a cost and therefore a liability, and the data have not convinced them otherwise. That is the essential purpose of this book, and it is the reason I keep reiterating the basic idea that treating people right pays off in real, hard numbers.

There is, however, one bit of good news: More and more senior financial executives (the ones who live and breathe numbers) see employees as a valuable resource rather than a cost, and they see people as key to performance, productivity, and share price. A 2004 study of 191 CFOs at major American corporations found that:

- 92 percent saw employee behavior as critical in achieving satisfied customers.
- 82 percent saw employees as having a large impact on profitability.
- 72 percent saw employees as key to achieving innovation and new products.[38]

In summary, organizations that are responsible socially, have a wide range of support for employees, and honor superior management practices, will have the highest levels of performance. This is not theory; the numbers prove it.

CHAPTER SIX

COMMITMENT AND ENGAGEMENT—*NOT* MORALE OR SATISFACTION

W HEN PEOPLE ARE ASKED, *"What do you do?"* they might say:

> *"I'm a software engineer,"* or
> *"I'm in finance,"* or
> *"I'm a professor."*

Or they might reply:

> *"I'm with Qualcomm,"* or
> *"I'm with CitiCorp,"* or
> *"I'm with the University of Michigan."*

If they answer by naming the organization where they work, chances are good that part of their identity and self-esteem comes from belonging to that organization. Their answer is a manifestation of *commitment*, one of the most critical elements for long-term organizational success.

When the organization they work for is a vital part of their sense of self, people are really involved—they are committed to that organization. Being part of that organization gives their lives meaning, purpose, and goals in which they believe. Because the organization is an important part of their lives, they want that affiliation to continue to be a source of pride. They want the organization to succeed, and they are willing to work hard and long to make that happen.

The other profoundly important ingredient for organizational success is employees' sense of *engagement*—a powerful, even passionate, dedication to the organization's mission and the things it accomplishes. Engagement is what causes people to say with pride, "What we do is really important, and what I contribute to this valuable work really matters."

Whatever the company's mission is, it has to capture the soul, the heart, and the mind of those who work there. Sometimes the mission is easy to position as extraordinarily valuable because it is self-evident that "We improve lives." In other instances the core value may be less obvious:

> "We lead in break-through technology."
> "Our manufacturing processes enable us to continue to
>   increase productivity."
> "We reward shareholders and employees."
> "We are a bastion of ethical behavior."
> "We protect intellectual freedom."

Professor Larry Smarr, Director of the Institute of Telecommunications & Information Technology, based in San Diego, put it this way: "When people think of San Diego I want them to think, 'That's where the future happens first.' "[1]

For another example, here's how The Four Seasons Hotels and Resorts, named one of *Fortune* magazine's consistent best places to work, has created a significant sense of mission for its employees and customers:

"MAKING LIFE FEEL PERFECT
FOR GUESTS EACH AND EVERY DAY
IS NO SMALL MIRACLE.
HERE'S TO
ALL THE MIRACLE WORKERS."[2]

The single best example of engagement I know came from a Navy SEAL who entered that elite unit after graduating from high school, stayed in for the term of his enlistment, and then left. Almost a decade later, he came back to the SEALs. When asked why he had returned he said, "Nothing else I did gave me the same sense of doing something really important and working with a great group of guys all of whom felt the same way. Each of us would die for the others. Not one of us would ever give up!"

Returning to the business world, Steve Peltier, CEO of Industrial Computer Source, explained his sense of his company's mission.[3] ICS manufactures computers designed to operate under harsh conditions; its mission was to become the number one industrial computer manufacturer in the world. Every single employee knew that achieving the mission would come from paying endless attention to customers, and thus the mission was an important part of creating meaning and direction for the employees.

At monthly companywide meetings, ICS's salespeople showed large photographs of particular customers and described, one by one, how ICS's computers made it possible for these customers to achieve critical and difficult objectives. These stories breathed life into ICS products and made every employee proud of the company and its machines. Every employee, therefore, was convinced that what they did really mattered, and that positive attitude created and sustained a strong sense of commitment and engagement.

NURTURING COMMITMENT
AND ENGAGEMENT

Commitment is what makes people say, "I'm proud to be working here; it's exactly where I belong." Engagement is what makes them say, "What we do matters. Let's go!" Just imagine what organizations could accomplish if all employees had that attitude.

Leaders of organizations who aspire to that level of passionate involvement might think in terms of a three-part strategy.

Ask the Right Questions

The first is to create and nourish a culture based on commitment and engagement. Ask yourself, your managers, and your employees these questions:

> What do we do as an organization that is a real source of pride for us?
> What happens to our people and our customers because of what we do?
> In what ways are we improving people's lives?
> What are our key values?
> Do we make sure that our leaders exemplify what we say we stand for?
> Do we 'walk the talk' and act in line with our values and mission?

A marvelous example of a deeply embedded cultural value is found in the Marine Corps motto, *Semper Fidelis,* which means "Always Faithful." *Semper Fi* declares that every Marine is engaged with every other member of this special group.[4] *Semper Fi* does not specify parameters of what needs to be done. Every Marine knows what it means and what it requires them to do.

When you ask those questions, pay close attention to the answers. Every resounding "yes" must become articulated and very visible throughout the organization. And every "no" calls for major change in terms of what is said and what people choose to do. Pursuing and achieving an organizational climate that supports commitment and engagement is so critical to future success that everyone's feet can be held close to the fire.

Hire the Right People

The second element is having the right people, those whose basic values, personalities, and temperaments fit naturally into a culture based on commitment and engagement. This means hiring the right people in the first place and getting rid of people who poison that culture.

Many of our young people are significantly different from their elders. Young boomers (aged 43 to 52 in 2007), GenerationX (25 to 42), and GenerationY (seven to 26) are different because they were not affected by the great economic depression.[5]

People who grew up in the shadow of the Depression (and it cast a huge shadow for about four decades) believe their priority of putting work first and becoming financially successful is a universal value. They're also convinced that compensation is the biggest reward, you can buy loyalty, and people are grateful to have a job. After all, that was true for almost everyone for all the years in which they grew up.

But, about half of employees today have nontraditional views, and their numbers are increasing.[6] Few nontraditional employees trust organizations and authority the way their parents did. Many of these younger employees are not loyal by the usual definition; they don't expect to stay with a single employer for the whole of their working life. And, increasing numbers of people, especially educated women, are choosing to work by themselves, independent of organizations.

When employees with new views join organizations, they want their commitments outside of work to be respected so there's some work–life balance. Partners may alternate who is most financially responsible for a particular period of time, and fathers as well as mothers insist on having hands-on time with their children. These nontraditional employees also want organizations to trust and respect them quickly based on what they contribute so they can have flexibility in where, when, and how they do their work.

These younger employees feel strongly that the work they do needs to make a significant contribution to something they value; they want people to be selected as managers largely on the basis of their interpersonal skills and leadership qualities rather than on their technical skills. Technology has been part of their lives for as long as they remember; connecting through IT and not face-to-face is comfortable for them. Nontraditional people want inclusive leadership in which different people's views, including their own, are given a serious hearing. In that light, they view managers largely as mentors rather than as bosses—and they will not work for managers who are arrogant and authoritarian, for whom formal status outweighs knowledge, creativity, and skill.

> Younger employees view managers largely as mentors rather than as bosses—and they will not work for managers who are arrogant and authoritarian.

Some organizations require job applicants to take standard personality tests; most Human Resources departments have a range of familiar instruments at their disposal. It may come as a new idea to some that these tests can be used to help determine who is, and is not, likely to fit into a culture of commitment and engagement.

In a 2006 study involving 3800 employees in different jobs in different industries, Development Dimensions International Inc. identified six personal characteristics shared by people who were likely to become highly engaged employees. They are emotionally mature, flexible, and highly motivated to achieve; they have positive attitudes, hold themselves to internal criteria of performance, and feel passionately about their work.[7] When people had a blend of these qualities, they were *14* times more like to become very engaged employees. Another interesting finding is that people who worked under supervisors who were engaged with their work were more engaged themselves and were 20 percent less likely to leave the organization within a year.

This means that personality tests that are probably already in place in the Human Resources area can give organizations valid tools for identifying those people who will contribute to, and fit in with, a culture of commitment and engagement.

The final element is a program of regular measurement, to monitor slippage and identify areas and people that need improvement.

Measure the Right Attributes

Employees with high levels of commitment and engagement are deeply involved in the organization, the work it does, and the goals it pursues. I reiterate this to make the point that commitment and engagement reflect *emotional* states, rather than rational, logic-based states. The opposite of engagement is nonengagement or, what is worse, active disengagement. The opposite of commitment is apathy. These negative feelings lead to alienation, anger, withdrawal, or depression. All these emotional states, negative as well as positive, have a powerful impact on the choices people make and the actions they take, and ultimately fuel a self-perpetuating cycle.

Organizations currently have tools to measure engagement and commitment, but they generally miss the emotional essence of these conditions. Standard questions just don't explore the feelings people are experiencing. The standardized questions too often suggest the "right" answer, and they don't provide any way for the person to describe the emotional component.

The only way to get below the surface and understand employees' emotional temperatures is to ask open-ended questions that allow respondents to say whatever they really feel. For instance, rather than "Is your boss fair?" ask "How would you describe your relationship with your boss?" This may mean either developing an entirely new instrument or amending the existing questions to elicit an emotional response.

To illustrate how much can be learned from the right kinds of questions, compare the following sets of answers. The questions are implicit, and the answers are hypothetical, but what they demonstrate is clear: Discerning what people *feel* provides much more valuable information about the organization than learning what they *think*.

Rational: My boss is fair and focuses on performance.
Actively Disengaged: My boss doesn't even know my name.
Committed and Engaged: I trust and admire my boss and I know she feels that way about me.

Rational: I have the tools and knowledge to do my job.
Actively Disengaged: I don't know what I'm supposed to be doing, and no one cares.
Committed and Engaged: My work is really important, so I make sure I really know what I'm doing so I get this stuff right.

Rational: I receive enough training so I can meet challenges.
Actively Disengaged: Our so-called training is Human Resource's way to increase its budget.
Committed and Engaged: My company keeps making it possible for me to become more and more valuable.

Rational: People in my group cooperate with each other.
Actively Disengaged: In my group everyone competes to get the few crumbs that are available.
Committed and Engaged: We are all joined together to get this done.

Rational: I am satisfied with my job.
Actively Disengaged: The only kick I get is showing up and doing nothing and getting paid.

Committed and Engaged: I would work here even if I didn't need the money.

Morale and Satisfaction Don't Count

Some readers may want to hold up their hand at this point and protest, "But we already do morale and satisfaction surveys. Isn't that the same thing?"

No, it isn't. Morale and satisfaction have become widely used assessments of a manager's performance, much more common than measures for commitment and engagement, but they are basically weak conditions of little note. In more than thirty years, organizational psychologists have never been able to confirm a relationship between employee satisfaction and business performance.[8]

What is worse, measurements of morale and satisfaction reinforce a sense of entitlement in employees or the presumption that people are owed what they get. Morale and satisfaction surveys are one-way streets. Typical questions ask, "Do you like your boss? Are you satisfied with your pay? Does your supervisor reward you enough?" These are measures of how *I* feel; how *I'm* rewarded; whether *I'm* satisfied.

There are no items on morale or satisfaction scales that ask whether or not employees are really earning whatever they get. The unstated inference is that the responsibility for satisfaction falls 100 percent on the organization, which owes its people comfort and happiness.

> No organization can afford a culture in which people feel they're owed. People need to earn the organization's positive responses through performance.

Traditional measurements of morale and satisfaction were, therefore, a wrong turning in the evolution of better management. No organization can afford a culture in which people feel they're owed. While it is in the organization's best interests to have employees feel supported, affirmed, respected, and liked, that has to be the result of employees' upholding their part of the deal. *Quid pro quo;* people need to earn the organization's positive responses through performance.

Just as important, organizations need to earn positive responses from their employees by responding to their people's core values. We've had two simultaneous basic changes: the economy changed, and so did many employees. The latter fact is as important as the former, but it is often ignored by leaders of most organizations.

Very briefly, and ignoring differences among people *within* a generation, while the views and core motives of the decision makers at the top of the organizational pyramid were shaped by the Great Depression, increasingly younger people don't share those views and perspectives.

These changes are explored in depth in Chapter 9. For now, an important corollary is that, considering this generational divide, senior executives may have to refine their definitions of real engagement. A young IT specialist may consider herself deeply committed to the organization and fully engaged in its mission, but may show it in ways that her older supervisor doesn't recognize.

That is another reason why standard, traditional measures of morale and satisfaction simply fail to assess what really matters.

GETTING IT WRONG

Commitment and engagement should be thought of as based on a mutual and interdependent relationship between the employee and the organization in which both are committed to each other; it is a two-way street. How the organization treats employees and how employees treat the organization reinforce mutuality and a commitment to a future together—or not.

It is staggeringly easy to destroy a sense of trust, respect, and mutuality.

In the spring of 2006, I ran into a friend I hadn't seen in a year. Ruth Anne is a banker in a local branch of one of the country's largest banks. After we had caught up on each other's latest activities and the fortunes of our many children, she said, "Judy, tell me again about this new subject you're working on."

It's a warning, I told her, a warning to organizations that unless their employees are committed and engaged, in the mid- and long-term they're going to do badly.[9] In plain words it means "Don't be penny wise and pound foolish." You need your employees to really care about their organization and their work so they bring energy, even passion, to what they do.

"Ruth Anne," I continued, "even though it's not a fashionable idea in an era of cost cutting, the data are really powerful in showing that management has to capture people's guts and hearts as well as their minds, or the financial results will be mediocre at best."

"That's what I remembered," she said. "And I tell you, I don't get it. We keep hearing about raising productivity but what I see is upper management putting the squeeze on our really experienced, knowledgeable people, trying to make things so uncomfortable that they quit. I understand that their salaries are higher than new people but when you look at productivity, we're losing it as those experienced people go."

"And," I added, "they're sending a lousy message: you can be a great performer but if your salary reaches a certain level, you're toast. That has to backfire. People will work just well enough to keep their job. But they won't jeopardize it by being ace performers who get bonuses and salary increases."

"That's another thing that bugs me," she said. "The economy is good and the bank is making money but they keep cutting our incentive pay. Every quarter we get a bonus depending on how many transactions we completed and when you're good, it starts to add up. So a few years ago, they cut it. Well, okay but then the next year and the next year they keep cutting it. So after a while you ask yourself why you're working so hard."

"You know, Ruth Anne," I said, "another bad thing management did was not explain their actions. If, let's say, they had said something like, 'We know our numbers are good despite increasing competition, but our stock price is lagging. We used to have the third highest share price in the industry but we've slipped into fifth place. If we cut costs and show an increase in profits there's a good chance the stock will go up. Since almost all of you own our stock, in the long run that would more than make up for any loss because we cut incentive pay.' That might have gone down okay. But not saying anything just breeds mistrust and the feeling, How are they going to screw us next time?"

Ruth Anne closed her eyes and silently nodded in agreement. After a moment she continued, "You're right. They're destroying any sense of trust in the bank or its executives that you might have had. How can we trust them when they're doing bad things to good people? Do they think we're stupid; that we don't know what's happening?

"All this is especially hard to explain because the bank takes commitment and entitlement very seriously. All of our managers have been trained to use and interpret Gallup's Q12 measure [see Chapter 4]. And woe to any manager whose branch doesn't keep getting better scores."

> How can we trust them when they're doing bad things to good people? Do they think we're stupid; that we don't know what's happening?

"I'm really sorry to hear what's happening to you guys," I said. "Your branch always had a great mood and even your temp tellers were always nice to deal with. It occurs to me that since about half of America's employees are either actively looking for a new job or they're seriously thinking about it, that it may have occurred to you and your colleagues that it's time to move on."

Again, Ruth Anne nodded in agreement. In a weary tone she said, "You're right. A lot of us are looking around. I hate that. I've been here for 22 years and it's a good bank and the pay is fair. But it's getting to where I don't like coming to work."

The result of the bank's short-term drive to get costs down has been a rash and needless waste of loyalty and trust, of commitment and engagement. The time and the cost to recapture those positive feelings will be dramatically greater than any savings the bank gained in the short term.

GETTING IT RIGHT

In light of the power of emotions to determine job performance, it is not surprising that

- High levels of employee commitment and engagement
- Lead to high levels of employee retention
- Which leads to high levels of customer enthusiasm[10]
- And high levels of customer retention and sales
- Which lead to higher profits and share price.

On the other hand,

- Non-engagement or active disengagement result in
- High levels of employee turnover
- Which results in widespread customer dissatisfaction
- And customer losses which results in
- Reduced sales, lower profits and falling stock prices.

The significantly different outcomes of powerful positive or negative emotions leads to one simple conclusion: Developing a culture that fosters mutual engagement and commitment between employees and management is an investment—not a cost —with a high rate of return.

CHAPTER SEVEN

CREATE SIGNIFICANT RELATIONSHIPS BETWEEN BOSSES AND SUBORDINATES

I N THE LATE 1980s, I had a lunch meeting with a Fortune 500 CEO whom I had never met. When I sat down at the table he turned to his associate and snarled, "So this is the book writer." It was not a compliment. He then grabbed my left forearm, pulled me close, and said, "In the year I've been here I've fired every executive but one. And now what I want to do is kill all those leeches, and I want you to tell them that." He was referring to his employees.

This man was abusive to me, and we were total strangers. We had no history, no animus, no relationship of any kind. There is no question what his style of leadership (and I use that word loosely) will produce in his subordinates—fear, then anger, then anxiety and a passionate desire to leave and go somewhere else, anywhere else.

A boss like this is comfortable tormenting and humiliating people, calling them stupid idiots in front of colleagues. This man apparently was in the right spot: A few years earlier I was at a management meeting with this same company when the man who was then CEO publicly told the entire Human Resources department that they were worthless and he'd be better off without them. (Oh, yes, the company was doing very badly when these two were in the top spot.)

Fortunately, this sort of behavior is now out of favor. Public, overt humiliation has become taboo at work, partly because of fears of employee lawsuits. Now, people who indulge themselves in savagery toward others are seen as out-of-control jerks who will cost the company big money in legal payouts or in lost commitment and high turnover. From a psychological standpoint, it is also clear that this kind of humiliation, including more subtle varieties that involve things like being ignored, is a breeding ground for thoughts of vengeance.

But more importantly, employees no longer stand still for it. Today the great majority of employees insist on being dealt with fairly, treated with respect, and acknowledged as being good at what they do.

We've always known that subordinates have to earn the respect of their bosses. Once upon a time that was essentially a one-way street, but no more. One of the biggest changes affecting management over the last half century is that in most organizations managers now have to earn the respect and trust of their subordinates. Unless an organization is very hierarchical, respect is no longer tied to a position. Today, the power to make decisions depends far less on status and hierarchical position and far more on trust and influence. The market for authoritarian leaders who treat employees with contempt is continuously shrinking.

> Today the great majority of employees insist on being dealt with fairly, treated with respect, and acknowledged as being good at what they do.

EMPLOYEE–BOSS RELATIONSHIPS

The single best way to learn how people feel about an organization is to ask them what they think of their boss. If they're gung-ho about the organization, they're invariably enthusiastic about their boss. But if they're lukewarm about their boss, they're just waiting to jump ship. People *join* companies, but they *leave* bad managers.

Relationships between bosses and subordinates should involve reciprocal trust and respect akin to that between a teacher and an able student. Of course the difference in decision-making power and responsibility can never be ignored; sometimes a boss must be a boss and give orders and deliver a critique. But that doesn't mean it's okay to humiliate a subordinate or manage through fear. Humiliation and fear are excellent breeding grounds for subversion and sabotage.

The data about relationships between employees and bosses are clear and powerful: employees are far more likely to make a commitment to the organization if they like and respect their boss and feel they are liked and respected in turn.

A Boss's Performance Is Directly Tied to Retention. [1]

- Only 11 percent of workers who rated their boss's performance "excellent" said they were likely to look for a new job in the next year, but
- 40 percent of those who rated their boss's performance "poor" said they were likely to jump ship.

The best relationships involve chemistry or rapport, which simply means liking someone and getting along easily. It means working with or for the other person is a positive experience that people look forward to.

One word of caution: These relationships can be friendly, but between boss and subordinate they don't involve friendship in the usual sense of that word. In friendships, people feel that they are peers despite differences in education or status or power. Friends don't judge each other, but a boss always has to make judgments about a subordinate's performance and abilities. Evaluating someone's present capacities and potential for additional responsibilities is a serious and on-going responsibility for management. Subordinates shouldn't forget that even a friendly boss is a boss.

Managers also have to coach their subordinates, which involves giving feedback. For feedback to be effective there has to be a preexisting relationship of mutual trust and respect.

Many managers are not comfortable managing *people* and prefer to view their responsibility as "hitting the *numbers*." But achieving the numbers requires the passionate enthusiasm of subordinates and that, in turn, depends on positive relationships between subordinates and managers and among team members.

At work today, we've learned that leadership and management require people to be emotionally or interpersonally intelligent. To lead and motivate people to continuously improve performance and create effective innovations, decision makers have to be able to inspire others, relate to them as individuals, and be trusted and respected by them. The obligation is mutual: Decision makers have to create opportunities for people to be able to earn others' respect and trust and a chance to be liked. There are no substitutes for respect and trust.

> We've learned that leadership and management require people to be emotionally or interpersonally intelligent.

THE SPECIAL IMPORTANCE OF TRUST

Trust is a huge asset; mistrust is a huge liability. When people operate from a place of trust, they're not using a lot of energy protecting themselves from abuse and manipulation. Without trust, people are defensive, cynical, and suspicious; this completely wipes out the possibility of collaboration. Mistrust, therefore, makes it almost impossible to achieve important change, a shared focus, and any sense of commitment and engagement. Trust, in contrast, leads to success; people who trust the organization, its leadership, and their boss are psychologically free to concentrate and collaborate.

Sometimes mutual trust is an outcome of being "honed on a hard stone," working together to prevent a mutual disaster by solving a hard and vital problem. In the summer of 2001, LTV's huge steel mill named Cleveland Works was bleeding red ink and staggering toward liquidation.[2] The number of employees had plunged from 18,000 to 3,200. The mill was failing on every dimension because it had not adapted to what had become a much more competitive industry. And the reason behind this nonadaptation was a long history of distrust between management and labor. A bankruptcy court judge ordered the plant to prepare to auction off its equipment.

Five years later Cleveland Works, now owned by Mittal Steel USA, is described by its employees as the most productive steel mill in the world. How did this happen? Relationships between labor and management did a complete reversal.

During the period when the plant was shut down, managers and workers realized they were experts in what *didn't* work. They knew that if the plant was to succeed, they needed to make a fundamental change in their relationship. Labor acknowledged that costs had to be cut, and management realized they needed the knowledge of workers. From adversaries, the Mittal executives and the United Steelworkers became partners. Relationships at the mill changed at the core, so they became really characterized by mutual listening, respect, and trust.

TRUST AND COMMUNICATION

Genuine trust depends on genuine communication, a process in which everyone involved really listens as well as speaks. But communicating is never simple, and that's especially true in relationships involving different levels of power. At that point what really counts is style: subordinates need to know what bosses and team members are comfortable with.

Every organization has an unwritten norm about confrontation and disagreement, and every employee needs to know what it is. And every boss has a very personal response to input, especially criticism. The great majority of executives I have worked with see agreement as loyalty and have a built-in push-back mechanism any time they encounter disagreement, especially in public. A good rule for subordinates is to make suggestions to executives in public and disagree in private.

Trust is created when people feel that someone's word is his or her bond and when they're told something will happen, it does. But even with the most honorable intentions this can be difficult, particularly in today's world, when the very rate of change makes it hard to predict and be consistent. Trust, therefore, depends on unusual levels of candor—an *open-book* culture—and on powerful values that everyone buys into. CarMax's CEO, Austin Ligon, for example, starts his Q&A sessions with employees by asking them to tell him anything the company is doing that is stupid or unnecessary, or just doesn't make sense.[3]

Trust is a great asset because it makes it easy to get people on board, but trust is based on "what you see is all there is," and that requires speaking up and effective communication. While transparency is a requirement for establishing trust, people frequently don't speak up in important personal or work relationships. They think total disclosure could be a bad idea, or they're afraid of looking foolish or alienating someone. Certainly it's important to always be aware of how much to say and how to say it, but the absence of honest communication *always* jeopardizes trust for the simple reason that if you don't speak out, people don't know where you're coming from.

> The absence of honest communication *always* jeopardizes trust.

Especially in today's fast-moving and extremely competitive environment, an organization's culture has to reinforce the necessity of speaking out in order to solve problems while really listening to the opinions of others. An open culture of speaking up and respectful listening invites participation and discussion. Then, any disagreement has a chance of becoming a situation in which different views are explored. When that happens, you get not only compromise and trust, but synergy and innovation.

Dishonest communication creates mistrust. Not speaking up at all is just as bad. Silence is destructive because it simply masks disagreements. Disagreements that are expressed have a good chance of being resolved. Unexpressed disagreements usually end up as heated conflicts. In fact, when people don't speak out to the boss about disagreements, they often do speak out in anger and frustration to their friends and allies. That usually leads to political in-fighting with employees taking sides. It's hard to imagine a worse outcome.

RELATIONSHIPS AT WORK

A friendly relationship at work means the people connect at a level that's comfortable for them. In all likelihood, it won't involve disclosure of anyone's deepest thoughts nor will it be totally honest because work is usually a political place.

There will also be great differences in the styles of how people connect. Many men use "male humor," short bits of sarcastic humor that are really cutting but are also really funny. Many women connect by telling stories about things that happened to them. And lots of people use charm and wit so they're fun to be around, but they're careful to never reveal anything like an opinion.

The best of relationships at work involve:

- Enough disclosure about where people stand so that others know enough to trust them and take them at their word.
- Enough empathy so people connect emotionally—they like and care about the other person.
- Enough admiration for people's skills and personal qualities so they know they're accepted.

- Enough commitment to the importance of good relation-ships so peer pressure and management directives don't allow anyone to be strongly narcissistic and manipulative.
- Enough good will and training so that really listening is basic to every conversation.
- Enough mutual respect so that disagreements are the begin-nings of discussions and not the ends of conversations.

OUT OF TOUCH WITH SUBORDINATES

We have a problem. The power of education, especially when it involves advanced degrees, has resulted in a troublesome trend: many managers and executives going straight from school into decision-making roles without ever having had experiences with the people who work in the offices or the plants. This is a form of class stratification in which people who are particularly good with abstract arguments or with information technology never work with—and thus never have the chance to gain respect for—the people who actually peform the work.

This pattern of putting people in leadership roles based on their mastery of theory and language is in strong contrast to the experiences of earlier generations of managers and executives.[4] The armed forces provide us with a very clear example.

Older business executives often served in the military when they were young because service was mandatory. Many of them came into service as newly commissioned officers straight from one of the military academies. They quickly learned that the success of their unit really depended on the decisions and actions of their very experienced noncommissioned officers. Experience taught the new graduate the critical importance of experiential knowledge, innate leadership abilities, and the astute decisions made by the people who reported to them. Actual experience and common sense trumped abstract theory.

Similarly, there was a time when many entry-level positions in management were in manufacturing facilities. Just as the brand-new second lieutenant learned how expert the master sergeant was, the brand-new manager quickly came to respect the foreman. Potential managers and executives swiftly learned that the DNA of the manufacturing processes was in the collective experience of the shop people who actually built the stuff. It didn't take the newly hired bosses long to realize that the people they were "to give orders to" were a tough audience with a dazzling understanding of everything that affected them. The new bosses swiftly learned that they couldn't survive—much less succeed—if they didn't earn the respect and support of their people.

In those earlier days, the route to success almost always involved tests of whether you could successfully lead all kinds of people. It was a humbling process for managers to realize how dependent they were on the knowledge, skills, and leadership abilities of people whose only difference was that they hadn't had the same educational opportunity. In effect, it was a reversal of the standard mentoring process in which your boss educates you.

This reverse mentoring meant new managers learned the language of the people who created value and made it certain that young managers would never underestimate the value or abilities of the people who reported to them. Along the way, the new boss learned that while people stood on different rungs of the ladder and had different roles, they were all part of a team in which every member contributed to their shared goal of success.

Today's organizations, by and large, have lost that advantage. The new generation of straight-from-business-school managers tend to be as convinced of their own indispensable contribution as they are unimpressed by the contributions of people they've never understood or worked with. Because they don't have personal relationships with less-educated people and they don't really work *with* them, too many contemporary managers and executives have no respect for those who report to them.

Without respect for subordinates, executives find it quite easy to think of employees as an expense to be managed. In that mindset, downsizing is a good thing and "Empower People" is merely a training program designed to thwart union organizers. When senior managers are blind to the value of subordinates and to their dependence on them, they are also blind to the high cost of thinking of employees simply as costs.

Too often, executives are also oblivious of the contributions made by middle managers. In 2004, as dozens of CEOs were fired, it was often middle managers who stepped up during the crisis and demonstrated their superior leadership qualities by getting products and services to customers and by being models of ethical behavior.[5] It is usually middle managers who interact every day with employees, customers, and suppliers, and thus they are the ones who know how the company is really doing. Executives can learn a great deal from them, and they need to give them much more respect and autonomy.

> It is usually middle managers who interact every day with employees, customers, and suppliers, and thus they are the ones who know how the company is really doing.

Let me tell you about two examples. The first involves Jeff McCracken, a middle manager and chief engineer with Norfolk Southern Railroad.[6] When Hurricane Katrina tossed five miles of railroad tracks into Lake Pontchartrain, Jeff was given the task of recovering or replacing them. After conferring with three bridge companies and dozens of engineers from Norfolk Southern, he decided to try to recover the track, as rebuilding would take weeks and totally paralyze transport to the West Coast.

To effect the recovery, Jeff pulled together a team of machine operators, other workers, and 365 company engineers. They worked in shifts around the clock to get everything in position. On September 12, just 14 days after the hurricane hit, the team lined up eight huge cranes. Using more than 400 tightly choreographed moves with heavy equipment, they lifted the five miles of track in a single piece and bolted it onto the bridge. Through all those efforts, involving many hours and using massive machinery, no one got hurt. That's extraordinary leadership.

The other example comes from my own experience. In the late 1970s, the University of Michigan began to require every decision-making committee to include students and nonprofessional staff. It was eye opening and occasionally shocking to professors to learn how smart and informed these "subordinates" were.

It is expensive and dangerous to allow management to minimize respect for the abilities and achievements of those who do not rise to their peer level. It is in an organization's best interests to create opportunities in which subordinates either participate as colleagues or as mentors to new managers and executives.

LEADERSHIP AND "AVERAGE" PEOPLE

Starting in the mid-1980s, the panacea for solving every economic and social issue was *leadership*.[7] Have a problem? Sprinkle on some leadership, and things will magically improve. As turbulence increased, the model of excellence, the ideal we all searched for, was the *heroic leader*—Jack Welch and Lee Iacocca, for example. They seemed able to find the most perfect solution and, in a top-down barrage of effective communication, they could bring the rest of the affected population on board.

Heroic leaders were and are necessary in periods of chaos and crisis. A command-and-control style of leadership may be very appropriate when there is a crisis, lots of red ink, failure and uncertainty, as existed during the 1980s. That's when we need heroic leaders. Why? Because they seem to know what to do, and they create a sense of hope in people who are scared. But that sort of top-down "messiah model" of leadership is not always the best choice.

With all the focus on leadership, few people noticed that in a period of escalating change, no one person at the top of the heap could possibly have solutions to problems at all levels and parts of an organization. Very few seemed to understand that a top-down—down-up bureaucratic form of communication was an unforgivable waste of time in a period when time was truly money.

If the time of our hero leaders has passed, who should we put in their place? How does an organization get the leadership it needs to thrive? The answer may be found in an unexpected quarter. Corporate America has a lot to learn from the armed forces.

The American military, especially the Marine Corps, has turned the concept of leadership on its head.[8] Just when corporate America largely abandoned its long-term commitment to its employees and demonstrated a lack of conviction in their employees' abilities, the U.S. military did exactly the reverse. Reviewing the new reality—a greater number of unknowns than known, instant communication anywhere in the world, warfare waged by loosely confederated groups of enemy instead of organized massed troops—the military decided that leadership would depend on the presence of leaders throughout their organizations.

> If the time of our hero leaders has passed, who should we put in their place?

The military creates this new breed of leaders by shaping "average" people into very successful performers. They operate on the premise that leaders can be found in all ranks and in all specialties; it only requires that people be given training to act as a leader and understand what leadership requires of them as individuals. Thus they invest in training and honing leadership skills *at all levels of the organization*.

The Marines are especially good at it. They have achieved extraordinary success in creating leaders and a culture of leadership throughout the organization because they genuinely believe in the potential of their members. The Marines also know that a "zero defects" mentality stifles boldness, so their culture expects and accepts reasonable mistakes.

The U.S. armed forces have defined the personal qualities that it takes to make decisions in an ever-changing environment of conflicting data and changing probabilities: intelligence and boldness, a willingness to act and take the initiative when you're not certain, an internal moral compass, and personal ideals and ideas you're willing to go all the way for. Is there a better definition of a real leader?

LEADERS FOR THE TWENTY-FIRST CENTURY

The messianic model of heroic leadership from the late twentieth century will not work in the twenty-first. The ideal style of leadership for today's organizations involves inclusion, greater personal responsibility, a greater sense of belonging, team collaboration, coaching and mentoring, and listening seriously to others' ideas because their knowledge and experience can enable them to make important and unique contributions.

The goal, it bears repeating, is to create a corporate culture of commitment and engagement, and these qualities rest on a foundation of *mutual* trust and respect. Giving people the opportunity to make contributions, to be successful, simultaneously demonstrates and earns respect, and sets the stage for increased commitment and engagement.

Employees need "yes" answers from management, notably their boss, to each and every one of the following questions:

- Do you need me?
- Do you recognize me?
- Will you reward me?
- Will you invest in me?
- Will you support me?
- Do you expect more from me?

When all the answers are affirmative, the response of people at all levels is "Count me in!"

CHAPTER EIGHT

STRENGTHEN THE BOND WITH EMPLOYEES BY CUSTOMIZING

H OW COMPANIES TREAT THEIR EMPLOYEES determines how committed and engaged the employees are.
Many leaders respond to this simple truth by touting
the "good-as-apple-pie" working conditions and rewards they
already have in place. I get it, they say smugly; look at what we're
doing.

The menu of apple-pie variables is well known. They are
espoused by almost every Human Resources expert and provided by almost all responsible organizations. The list includes:

Competitive compensation and health and pension
    benefits.
Tuition assistance.
Life insurance.
Profit sharing and stock options.
Admirable leadership.

Good communication.
A vision and mission workers can identify with.
Teamwork.
Training and retraining.
Counseling and coaching.
A flexible work–life arrangement

But how much do people really value these things? Two recent studies looked at a broad range of practices that HR people typically consider motivators to discover which factors actually meant the most to the largest number of workers. Every single business leader and every Human Resources specialist needs to heed the results. In one study, the greatest impact of any single variable was 14 percent; in the other, it was 10 percent. In both studies, the category that had the *most* impact was "all other factors" (See Tables 8.1 and 8.2).[1]

Table 8.1
"None of the Above," Part 1

Gaining Employee Trust Relies on Seven Key Factors

1. Explaining reasons behind major decisions	10%
2. Gaining support for the business direction	10%
3. Motivating workforce to high performance	10%
4. Promoting the most qualified employees	10%
5. Acting on employee suggestions	9%
6. Providing job security	9%
7. Encouraging employee involvement	8%
8. **All other factors**	**34%**

(Reprinted with permission from WorkUSA 2000 – Employee Commitment and the Bottom Line(c) 2006, Watson Wyatt Worldwide. For more information, visit www.watsonwyatt.com)

Table 8.2
"None of the Above," Part 2

Key Drivers of Employee Commitment

1. Trust in senior leadership	14%
2. Chance to use skills on job	14%
3. Competitiveness of rewards	11%
4. Job security	11%
5. Quality of company's products/services	10%
6. Absence of work-related stress	7%
7. Honesty and integrity of company's business conduct	7%
8. **All other factors**	**28%**

(Reprinted with permission from WorkUSA 2000 – Employee Commitment and the Bottom Line(c) 2006, Watson Wyatt Worldwide. For more information, visit www.watsonwyatt.com)

The message here is, don't assume that what you are already doing is what your employees need and want. Don't assume that what you already have in place for a large group of employees will be satisfying for the individuals within that group.

> No single change has the power to create commitment and engagement for an entire group of people.

We might think that the way for sagging companies to increase commitment is to give employees more of these items, to change the offerings in some way. The organization is, after all, in control of those factors and can change them at any time. But the reality is that no single change has the power to create commitment and engagement for an entire group of people. There is no magic bullet that works for everyone.

However, a single intervention can be enormously powerful in changing the attitudes and behaviors of an *individual* if it gives people what they most need or want *now*. I believe this is the key to increasing employees' passionate commitment to the company's success.

Paying attention to the priorities of individuals sounds like an impossible task because of the sheer number of possible preferences. In fact, in reality it doesn't work out that way. Although it is true that priorities can and do change with different economic conditions or life stages or technology requirements, the priorities of individuals always fall into a relatively small number of clusters at any one time.

After my book *The Plateauing Trap* was published in 1986, I gave lectures on that subject to many thousands of people.[2] I would ask members of the audience to call out answers to the question, "What do you need from your work in order for you to feel satisfied?," and I would write their answers on flip charts or a blackboard.

It was not unusual to have 30 to 50 different responses. But those responses could almost always be clustered into four groups:

Money and other extrinsic rewards

Opportunities for challenge, which involved continuous learning and manageable risk

Empowerment, which involved greater autonomy and decision-making authority

Opportunity to do significant work and be treated as a significant contributor

Money, challenge, empowerment, and significance—four clusters of preferences is a very manageable list.

There seems to be a natural limit to the variety of outcomes that achieve a high priority at any moment. To the question, What do you most need or want *now*, there are relatively few answers.

In my lectures in the decade from roughly 1985 to 1995, the first audience response to the question was always "challenge"; "money" was never called out until we already had about a third of the total list. In the years from 1995 to 2002, the two leading responses were money and autonomy. The lesson here is that what really differentiates people is *when* a person wants a particular condition or outcome.

HUMANIZE THE WORKPLACE

The basic idea of customization is to create a cafeteria of options that individuals can choose from. The items on the menu must be compatible with the organization's values and, of course, there needs to be a financial ceiling. Once a year or once every several years, employees select the specific items that are most important to them at that time. This program of outcomes and conditions can then be customized for individual workers.

The first step involves asking questions and listening to the answers. You need to find out what employees' priorities are, not generally but in very specific terms. At the end of this chapter you will find an extensive menu of possible items; they are meant as suggestions only, as an aid to structuring the discussion in your particular organization.

It's important to solicit input from both the employees and their managers, so that the end result is both meaningful and realistic. By the way, really listening and relating to an individual employee is also, in itself, a powerful demonstration that the employee's well-being and preferences are important to the organization.

The second step involves an active discussion between employees and their managers in which options are created and choices are made based on their importance to the individual and their feasibility.

To construct the clusters in any particular organization, it is not necessary to interview each and every employee. A representative sample is usually sufficient. How many interviews does it take? In a large organization, about 100. You know you have sufficient data when the interviews are no longer providing new information.

After a sufficient sample of interviews has been held, the basic clusters can be identified and individual entries can be assessed as to feasibility and value within the organization. They are then either assigned to a cluster, or discarded.

Every few years, the organization should repeat this process. Interview a substantial sample of people again and determine whether priorities are changing. At the same time, perhaps even annually, assess the program's effectiveness from two sides:

1. What effect has it had on employee commitment and engagement?
2. What about financial outcomes? What were the effects on:
   Employee and customer retention
   Sales
   Profitability
   Share price
   Return on equity

To make this work, the conditions and outcomes that people can earn need to be in line with both the employee's priorities and the organization's values. They must be effective, and they need to be affordable.

The choices that people make should generally be binding for some designated period of time, after which their choices can change. However, it's a good idea to also incorporate some flexibility, because it further demonstrates the organization's commitment to an employee's well-being.

Don't let yourself get bogged down in endless discussions of what conditions or outcomes employees can earn. The list of offerings will naturally evolve over time just as an individual's priorities will.

Most of all, remember that the specifics of what people can earn are often less important than the message delivered by what the organization actually does. That message is: your performance is crucial to our success and therefore we are not going to take you for granted, ignore you, or casually discard you.

In a nutshell, "Humanize the Workplace" simply means to pay attention to the people who do the work. This is not kindness; it is at the heart of being able to succeed and be profitable.

FAIR—BUT NOT IDENTICAL

A few years ago, I delivered a talk to an audience of Human Resources specialists. One of the observations I made was that baby boomers and Gen-Xers had a wider range of core motives than did the older Depression-affected generations for whom security was the number-one motivator. As a result, I said, those of us involved in HR issues will need to pay attention to what individuals want.

"But that wouldn't be the same for everyone," one participant protested, "and that wouldn't be fair!"

Fair does not have to mean *identical*. While that's a pretty easy idea to grasp, in practice it's a really radical statement. We start learning that fair does mean identical when we are very young and our teachers carefully divide a treat so that every child gets exactly the same amount. Giving one child more than another would be favoritism, and we know that gets even little kids really angry and upset. Favoring one child over another would also require thinking through why one kid deserved to get more and another less.

Historically, our schools, governments, and corporations have talked about treating people differently on the basis of performance, but in practice they treat most everyone in the same rank or the same job or the same level of seniority the same. There are benefits to this approach. First, it makes fairness self-evident, while also reducing the legal liabilities of discrimination. More importantly, treating everyone the same reduces the need to deal with people and their individual performances and preferences.

Organizational leaders need to shake loose of this idea of absolute fairness. A lot of very valuable new research highlights the differences among generations. Most of the time the differences show up as a preference in one generation that is not shared by people in other generations. But for organizations, the difference among generations should probably be thought of as the difference in the percentage of people in any group for whom a particular outcome or working condition is especially important.

It's reasonable to assume, for example, that everyone would prefer to do work that they find meaningful. It is really interesting, in fact, to see how people in basically mundane occupations, like collecting road or bridge tolls, are able to perceive their work as helping others. This view enables them to see their work as meaningful.

> Organizational leaders need to shake loose of this idea of absolute fairness.

But when we look at the question from the perspective of generations, we find that while almost all of the Depression-affected employees would prefer their work to be meaningful, only a small percentage would consider that a requirement. In contrast, meaningful work might be a required component for about a third of the older boomers, half of the younger boomers, and perhaps 80 percent of GenXers.

INVOLVING EACH EMPLOYEE INDIVIDUALLY

Differences among generations offer vital clues as to what the majority of any group wants, and that information reveals major social changes. But that level of information does not tell us what an individual prefers. It is, therefore, useful to *think* in terms of demographic differences but *act* in terms of individual preferences.

Which leads to the question, *Do we have to treat people as individuals?* Because that philosophy is likely to have a large payoff in terms of positive feelings and behaviors, it is an inherently good idea. But when your workforce includes younger boomers and GenXers and anyone else who holds their individualism dear, you have no choice. You *must* treat them as individuals because for them individuality is a core value.

Keep in mind that people's priorities don't always hinge on their cost. Business organizations tend to assume that the major motivators for everyone are compensation and status. Those are extrinsic motivators, which means that satisfaction comes from something outside the work itself. This simply means that some people will do work they dislike if it offers enough money, security, recognition, or power. Other kinds of organizations, such as universities and not-for-profits, believe people are mostly motivated by intrinsic motivators, such as opportunities to keep learning and work that makes a difference, in which the biggest payoff comes from doing the work.

While it used to be true that people put more weight on either extrinsic or intrinsic payoffs, lately many people want both. Even highly compensated people want their work to give them the opportunity to keep learning and meet new challenges while they're doing work that matters. And fueled by the heady money that was made in the heyday of the dot-com era, even people who put intrinsic payoffs first can now appreciate how compensation can make life easier. Organizations should pay attention to both intrinsic and extrinsic rewards and enable employees to earn both.

Also, keep in mind that people's priorities change as their lives change and their responsibilities increase. That's why I recommend that organizations revisit their program every one or two years. Ask the question again: What's most important to you at work right now and for the next one [or two] years? Keep asking: You cannot enable people to satisfy their most important needs if you don't know what they are.

One final caution: Remember that you cannot promise that all employees will be able to earn their singular preferences. Never promise anything you're not certain you can deliver. Broken promises destroy trust, and once trust is gone, it is very hard to rebuild.

TODAY'S CLUSTER OF PRIORITIES

Fortunately, most of the priorities of individuals will fall into a reasonably small number of clusters and that makes it relatively easy to identify them and make them operationally available.

Many of the familiar priorities from the past 20 years are still valuable. People want to:

• Keep learning.
• Achieve reasonable security.
• Be successful.

But some are new. Today's workers also want to:

• Have both my work and my family flourish.
• Like and respect my colleagues and bosses.
• Find meaning in my life and my work.

Within those clusters, it is possible to draw up an extensive menu of choices so that each and every employee can find things he or she values. At the end of this chapter, you will find many suggestions. Reading through them may trigger other ideas. Of course, not all items will be applicable to any one organization. Every organization needs to customize its offerings according to its values and the values of the workers it wants to hire and retain.

In short, within realistic possibilities and limits, individual employees should be able to earn the conditions and outcomes that matter most to them at any given time.

Yes, developing a new program like this takes time. But the cost/payoff ratio is terrific. Organizations can afford to be psychologically flexible and generous to employees who have earned generosity through their sustained excellent performance. I'll say it more bluntly: If you want to retain that level of excellent performance, you can't afford not to.

MANAGE TO SUCCESS: CUSTOMIZE RECOGNITION

To maximize the effect of customization, organizations should also customize how they praise and reward employees and that should involve and affect how employees are recognized.

Organizations need to *manage to success,* which means they do everything possible to help employees succeed. The reason is simple: nothing motivates people as much as success. Managing to success also involves praise and recognition. Again, customization is key. Truly effective rewards require managers to really know their people so they can select meaningful outcomes.

When it comes to praise and recognition, two errors are common. The first involves Scrooge-like behavior, which means withholding any positive response in the face of excellence. Managers frequently justify this error by proudly declaring, "I don't need praise from anyone!" Whether that's true or not is irrelevant; what matters is that it's lousy management. When people have achieved something significant, especially if it was against high odds, they expect some kind of positive response, and they've earned it. It is true that people usually derive intrinsic satisfaction from knowing that they succeeded, especially

> Nothing motivates people as much as success.

when the task was difficult, but people also revel in the organization's recognition of their outstanding performance.

The other error is the opposite: doling out so much praise and recognition that they have no value. Devaluing recognition is pretty common in large organizations, especially those that have gone so far as to have a Department of Recognition. Then, recognition is formalized and bound up in rules rather than ribbons.

Over time, recognition specialists can become paralyzed because of philosophic issues like, "Different jobs have different levels of visibility, and it's much easier for some people to get noticed than others." To undo this painful inequity, the recognition specialists have been known to enlarge the opportunities for everyone to "earn" recognition.

My personal favorite was the utility in which employees could nominate people for a recommendation because that person had been nice to them. Of course, that was not surprisingly generous because that was also the organization in which people could nominate themselves for recognition. The hurdles to recognition in that company were so low that recognition had become a joke.

Timing is important. Recognition is most powerfully effective when it is delivered very soon after the accomplishment. A letter of praise from the CEO written a few days after a project was finished is far more meaningful than attending a recognition banquet three months later.

Also, the recognition that is savored and remembered rarely involves a lot of money. Mostly, the recognition that really matters is personal, spontaneous, heartfelt, and delivered by someone who really knows the work and the people involved.

I recently asked participants in a training class to tell the group the recognition that they remembered as being the most meaningful. Here are some of their responses:

- Three years after I completed a project, my former boss said, "Remember Project X? That was a really nice job you did." (It was important to me not for its timeliness, but because this was a person who never gave compliments.)

- Being cited as an expert by a speaker in front of an audience of 300-plus peers and superiors.
- Contractor threw a significant thank-you celebration for enabling their work.
- Being offered two jobs even when the number of candidates was large.
- Verbal and written recognition before my whole team.
- Comments from peers, management, and subordinates regarding what people "liked" about me at an off-site organizational effectiveness meeting.
- My senior vice president recognizing/commenting on my efforts (re: a project) to 150 people in a banquet setting.
- Letter from the president and a promotion.
- Being allowed to take on extremely influential assignments or roles.
- Receiving praise from a manager that few could please.
- E-mail note from a customer listing each member of one team and what they did, with copies to the whole business unit.
- High-level manager took me to dinner.
- Twenty-five dollar Macy's gift certificate for one year's perfect attendance.
- Visit in hospital by vice president. I was employed less than two years.
- Way-To-Go Award telling me I did an excellent job.
- Took a training class for a week that allowed me to travel. Not a local class.
- A peer of my boss knew of some of my achievements and mentioned them to me.
- Being asked to lead a work group at a trade organization.

Here's my own story. The most memorable recognition I ever received was a vase of flowers delivered to me by Billy Frye, then the dean of the College of Literature, Science, and the Arts at the University of Michigan when I was an associate dean. It was not my birthday, not the anniversary of the day I became a dean, and it was not "Recognize Your Subordinates" day. Billy had walked blocks in Michigan's winter to get to the florist and then blocks to my office in order to give me a spontaneous gift that basically said, *"Thanks!"*

In summary, letting people earn the working conditions, assignments, and outcomes that they need or want at this time and managing to success by celebrating and recognizing their accomplishments are well worth the effort. They go a long way in capturing and fostering commitment and engagement.

SUGGESTIONS FOR CUSTOMIZATION MENU ITEMS

Organizations should aim to construct a menu of choices in each category that are meaningful to employees and that also reflect the organization's values. The items listed here are merely suggestions. Each organization will select ones that are especially relevant and should feel free to add others. In this list, the items I think are particularly important or creative are **in bold**.

I want to: keep learning

- **Work that's different in content, place, or responsibility**
- **Challenges that involve some risk**
- **Advanced professional education**
- **A customized career that develops a whole range of professional skills**
- **Assignments that develop interpersonal skills**
- **Experiences that increase self-knowledge**
- Periodic sabbaticals to expand the breadth of my experiences
- Training
- Mastering new knowledge and skills

- New assignments
- Mentors and coaches available
- New leaders are put through a development program.
- Funding and time to participate in professional meetings
- Reimbursement for going to professional meetings or courses
- Professional dues and publications paid
- Tuition paid in full or partially
- Lecturers are brought to the organization.
- College classes on site

I want to: achieve reasonable security

- **Job security conditional on whether the organization needs what I do and can afford to pay me and whether my performance and attitude are excellent**
- **Clear expectations and outcomes**
- **Vacations, salaries, and benefits cut before any major layoffs.**
- **Continuous collaboration to improve performance and keep work in-house.**
- **Hiring and promotions based on merit and involve peer review as well as assessment by bosses**
- **Career counselors available to help employees increase their value to the organization**
- Adequate and relevant training and education
- Periodic wage and benefit increases
- Bonuses and stock options tied to individual, team, and company performance
- Pay for achieving goals, having the right attitudes, and treating others with respect
- A policy of no layoffs
- Bias and discrimination severely punished
- Employees not perceived as disposable
- A long-term commitment to employees
- Affordable and portable health and dental insurance with costs shared by the organization and employees

- On-site medical and wellness centers
- Choice of medical plans, including flexible spending accounts up to $5,000 to pay for healthcare deductibles and other health items like routine physicals, over-the-counter drugs, exams, and eyeglasses
- Paid sick leave
- Choice of dental plans
- Choice of life insurance plans
- Choice of retirement finances [pension, IRA, 401(k)]
- Long-term care insurance
- Disability insurance
- Portable pensions
- Defined benefit pensions
- Low-cost loans
- Spouse receives employee's retirement pay
- Domestic partner benefits
- Flexible age-related retirement policies
- Compensation for commuter costs, including parking and mass transit fees
- Individual Retirement Accounts that are owned and managed by employees with help from financial advisers
- Safety on the job is a major goal

I want to: be successful

- **Significant amounts of merit compensation**
- **Acknowledgment in the form of opportunities to lead and make decisions**
- **Opportunities to be entrepreneurial and create new projects or businesses**
- **Acknowledgment of my contributions to my profession and my community**
- **Leadership flourishes throughout the organization.**
- **New positions created to accommodate special talent**
- **Major forms of recognition at all levels and functions**

- Recognition and rewards, both symbolic and monetary
- Travel and merchandise awards
- Increased autonomy
- Opportunities to "be at the table" with the decision makers
- Opportunities to control, use, or invest increasingly large sums of money
- Individualized compensation includes profit sharing, bonuses, 401(k)s, and shares or stock options
- Bigger challenges
- Individualized working conditions
- Individualized recognition
- Individualized compensation and benefits
- Coworkers vote on potential new employees
- A private office
- An active support network
- An ombudsman to handle employee issues
- A peer-elected committee giving lower-ranked employees a voice
- Promotions and compensation determined by a panel of peers and not by manager
- Health coverage and tuition reimbursement for part-time employees
- Employment opportunities or tuition allowances for spouses on international assignments
- 10 percent of the first year's cost savings to the employee who suggested the idea
- Creative freedom to devote one-fourth of time to pursue work-related ideas outside of regular work
- Onsite MBA program free with grades of A or B, half off if grade C.

I want: my work and my family to flourish

- **The basic value that healthy family relationships are an asset to the business**
- **Respect and consideration for dads as well as moms**

- **Agreed-upon rules in regard to employee accessibility**
- **Ability to earn a partnership or tenure while working less than full time**
- **Cutting-edge communication tools so I can work anywhere, any time**
- Short-term family leaves and assistance for child and elder care
- Help with disabled family members
- More time off
- Flexibility about career interruptions for outstanding employees
- Training and education available for employees during a period of career interruption
- Mentors or coaches, and part-time jobs or assignments, for employees during a period of career interruption
- On-site services that minimize time spent running errands
- On-site services for child and elder care or referrals to excellent and affordable care
- Flexibility about when and where work is done
- Shared jobs
- Training for managers in managing distributed workers
- Work schedules that minimize the number of times employees have to choose between work and family
- Employee works only during school year
- Work/family programs
- Healthy lifestyle programs
- Longer parental leave than legal minimum
- Full to part-time work
- Managers trained to support employees who work at home
- Flex-time, compressed work weeks, and flex-place
- Reimbursement for child care expenses
- Paid family leave
- Unpaid family leave
- Opportunities for telecommuters and part-time employees to participate in significant projects
- Managers who stay in touch with employees who leave for a number of years

- Meetings held when everyone can come (i.e., during lunch hour)
- Flexibility about where people live
- Adoption assistance
- Same-sex-partner coverage
- Programs directed at men as well as women
- Saturday child care
- 20 days of free back-up care for all kids and another extra 20 days for kids aged three to six months
- 24-hour child care
- Time to visit your child's classroom
- Elder care program, including counseling
- Summer camps
- A parents' night out
- A paid week off for new grandparents
- On-site afterschool programs

I want to: like and respect my colleagues and bosses

- **Hire great people**
- **Select managers based as much on their ability to lead and interact with people as on their professional skills.**
- **Rewards for effective development of subordinates**
- **An organization that encourages a sense of belonging and community**
- Strong values about sharing what one knows, so teamwork is a natural outcome
- An "open-book" culture in which employees as well as managers know what is happening
- A culture where people tell the truth because the truth is respected and expected
- Management that is accessible and trained to listen to employees' input
- Competition directed at the competition, so peers can be colleagues
- Activities to build a community at work
- Knowledge respected in decision making
- Walking the talk is key

- People are expected to be responsible.
- People are expected to share what they know.
- People are expected to speak out.
- A flat playing field
- Collaboration is expected.
- A CEO who has lunch with every new hire

I want: my life as well as my work to have meaning.

- **Work that contributes to causes or outcomes that I really value**
- **Employees have opportunities to see the difference their work makes.**
- **The sense I'd still work here even if I won the lottery**
- **The perception the world would be worse off if we didn't do our work**
- The organization is passionate about new ideas.
- Paid time off to volunteer at organizations whose work I believe in
- The culture doesn't punish reasonable mistakes
- Voluntary shared-leave programs
- Charitable matching donations
- Technology makes work more fulfilling.
- People can achieve closure at work.
- Employees are expected to have input.
- Unnecessary work is eliminated.
- The company occupies a socially responsible niche.
- Employees help to choose the work they do.
- There are opportunities to see the effects of the employee's or company's work.
- A six-month sabbatical (with full pay) to pursue a project that will benefit the company or community in a meaningful way

Miscellaneous Suggestions

- Employees can mail packages on site at the holidays at the company's discounted rates

- Food gifts at Thanksgiving and Christmas
- Hot-lines to help employees quit smoking, manage diabetes, lose weight, get psychological counseling, find child care, receive coaching for legal and financial issues, and get health risk assessments
- ATMs and postage machines on-site
- Bagels, muffins, coffee, tea, and water on-site
- Cafeteria on-site
- Taxi or limo transportation home after late hours
- Company negotiates low rates for long-term-care insurance, vision care, auto loans, cell phone plans, and computers that employees can purchase.
- Cleaned and pressed uniforms or laundry service
- Good meals at discounted cost at company facilities
- Free stays at company's hotels
- Free or cut-rate airline tickets
- Free limos for weddings
- Family-style kitchens with meal service
- Massages
- A meditation and/or yoga and/or nap room
- Friday cocktail hour
- A seasonal farmers market
- On-site gym, including a basketball court
- Sports teams, hayrides, ski trips
- Lower-level employees get higher profit-sharing percentages than highly compensated employees
- Tickets to events
- Lavish parties to celebrate a major success
- Professionally made take-home dinners
- Cruises on the company yacht or rides in company helicopter
- Handsome buildings in lovely settings
- Posters of employees mounted on walls
- College-age children or grandchildren receive 100 percent of tuition, up to $20,000 per year, if they maintain a GPA of 2.5 or higher
- Paid vacation trips

- Full service on-site dentist
- Matches for charitable donations
- Generous referral bonuses
- Periodic on-site driver's license renewals
- Bring dogs to work
- Performances of live music by employees at lunch time
- A putting green
- Free fishing classes and equipment to use during breaks
- An extra week's vacation and $500 on your wedding day

CHAPTER NINE

ACHIEVE A BEST FIT

IN 2004 MY SON, PETER, was interviewing for the position of chief financial officer in a young start-up company. He did well in the interviews and was one of the two finalists. "The other guy is actually more qualified than I am," Peter told me, "but I think I have an edge because he's only worked in Fortune 100 companies." Peter, on the other hand, had lots of experience with young companies; his last three positions had been at start-ups. And he was right: he got the job.

He got the job because he was a Best Fit. His particular mix of personal characteristics, attitudes, work habits, priorities, values, preferences, and so on dovetailed nicely with the requirements and attributes of the company. And this company was savvy enough to recognize that those personal qualities were more important than specific job experience.

Best Fit means there's a good match between what an individual requires or desires and what the organization can offer.

The person who relishes the risks and challenges of a start-up will find the rules and bureaucracy of a very large organization stifling. Similarly, the person who is comfortable working in a Fortune 100 company has a certain package of expectations and requirements, and they simply cannot be fulfilled in a two-year-old start-up.

With Best Fit the goal is to create a match between the core culture of the organization and its stated and *unstated* requirements and expectations on one hand, and the personal qualities and priorities of the individual on the other hand. So much of any working environment is subtle and unstated. If new employees have a personality that aligns with the company's culture, they can slide right in and become productive without having to fight against the discomfort of a mismatch they may not even have a name for.

Put simply, Best Fit is critical to success, both for the individual and the organization. It is what enables people to truly thrive, to do their very best—or not.

HIRING FOR BEST FIT

Most of the time, our corporations do not give enough consideration to the question of Best Fit during the hiring process. People are usually hired because they have the relevant knowledge and skills for the job; the presumption is that they can begin to contribute to the organization immediately. But the concept of Best Fit says those are the wrong criteria on which to hire. Regardless of education or experience, ultimately it's personality, values, and attitudes that will determine whether or not someone will succeed. Best Fit says that you should not hire someone who will not fit in, even if that person has the relevant experience and skills.

Different organizations have different values and cultures that fit best with certain people and not others. At the same time, potential employees display a great breadth in personal characteristics. This means that there is room for all types. It's not a question of better or worse, right versus wrong. It's simply a question of putting the right person in the right spot in the right organization.

Creating Best Fit means searching out people who are likely to fit into the organization as it is or as it will be, and whose most important needs and priorities can be met. No matter how valuable a person's skills, experience, and intelligence could be to an organization, it is a bad idea to bring that someone in if their personality, work style, or preferred working conditions are not a match. You simply waste too much valuable time trying to force square pegs into round holes.

Employees have to feel that they connect in the organization because people cannot succeed unless they fit in. "Fitting in" refers to a sense of ease, a positive chemistry. People much prefer to work with others with whom there is an easy connection. This means that selecting the right people and letting go of the wrong people are more important than experience, training, or mentoring where core personal qualities, attitudes, and work habits, and values and expectations are involved. In short, there needs to be a Best Fit from the get-go.

> Selecting the right people and letting go of the wrong people are more important than experience, training, or mentoring.

It may come as a surprise to some executives that their interviewing skills are not up to the task of eliciting information about a candidate's core personality. In a recent study, 44 percent of managers reported that job candidates' personality in an interview was really different from what those people were like on the job.[1] Imagine that: people put their very best foot forward in the artificial environment of an interview. Interviewing has never been a very valid measure of attitudes and values. An interview is basically an assessment of personality, charm, and charisma. It does not usually measure character, values, and the level of risk the candidate is comfortable with.

To find their Best Fit, then, organizations need to know what is most important to them in terms of what they expect from people, and they need to know which personal qualities characterize the people who succeed within their organization—or don't. It's best if an organization uses valid personality tests and develops interview techniques that dig deeper into an applicant's personal characteristics. One good place to start is the two questionnaires I developed, one for companies and one for individuals, that you will see later in this chapter.

MANAGING TO SUCCESS

When all aspects of the organization's Human Resource policies are aimed toward the common goal of helping all employees succeed at their jobs and therefore ultimately bring success to the company, we can say that the organization is "managing to success."

It starts with hiring people who will fit in and will, therefore, be comfortable and productive very quickly. Managing to success also means creating opportunities for people to broaden their work and interpersonal skills by mixing different people together on challenging and important projects. When good workers are invited to participate in new initiatives with different people, they learn to listen and collaborate. Another benefit is that morale is likely to be heightened, as people realize they are no longer pigeon-holed into one narrow capacity, something most people resent. And not incidentally, the probability of achieving significant breakthroughs is greatly increased.

When people are given a range of challenging opportunities there is a good chance that, over time, they will demonstrate increasing judgment and maturity, develop latent talents which had not been previously visible, and show the ability to lead. In other words, they will earn various forms of success.

Success is the ultimate energizer, and the organization's success is one key reason why people choose to work and stay there. When people recognize that they and their organization are flourishing, the potential for engagement and commitment is enormous. And when people are both engaged and committed, there is no limit to what they can accomplish.

REALLY KNOW
EXPECTATIONS AND PRIORITIES

For much of the twentieth century, the number-one priority for the great majority of working Americans was security. It was the lingering, multigenerational impact of the Depression. Workers who were born long after the Depression grew up hearing the cautionary tales of older relatives or neighbors. Perhaps they watched as the town's main factory closed and many people lost their wages, benefits, and pensions.

Even young people who never directly experienced the Depression shared the majority view that achieving security was the main goal. If that was accomplished—the man of the house got a job with a big company and could expect to stay there forever—people might then strive for some success and a comfortable life.

Because of the universality of this view, people were far more alike than individualistic. They mostly wanted the same things. At the same time, the great majority of American organizations were also far more alike than different. They were based on the traditional hierarchical pattern that hadn't changed much in more than a century. So they were predictable providers of the patterns of security that most people were seeking.

Now, in the beginning of the twenty-first century, both are undergoing profound changes. Organizations are showing a far broader range of characteristics, and employees display a far wider range of individual qualities. In the world of work, we are quickly becoming more different than we are alike.

While many fundamental economic conditions have been changing since the 1970s, they are changing at different rates in different places and in different industries. Even within the United States, there is a broad range of basic economic conditions in various parts of the country and in different industries. This means there is also a broad range of practices, values, and expectations among different organizations.

Organizations are changing, and so are the people who work in them. Companies can no longer assume that what their workers want in terms of things such as working conditions, risk level, flexibility, autonomy, accessibility, work–life balance, and the like will be the same for all employees. We are seeing major demographic differences and a greater insistence on individuality than we ever saw in the twentieth century.

> We are seeing major demographic differences and a greater insistence on individuality than we ever saw in the twentieth century.

Organizations will do well to heed these changes and pay attention to the new priorities that employees bring with them. Losing, recruiting, rebooting, and retraining are very costly. Organizations need to know themselves and hire with caution.

Potential employees have a comparable responsibility. They need to learn everything they need to know about an organization's values and expectations before they agree to become a member of it, and they must honestly weigh those expectations against their own priorities and values.

THE QUESTION OF RISK

When working toward Best Fit, one of the most critical things to consider—probably more important than anything else—is the question of risk. It's a two-way question, relevant for both the organization and prospective employees. What is the basic risk level of the organization? And how does the employee feel—*really* feel—about risk: enjoy it, merely tolerate it, or fear it?

Many people are risk avoiders. They need reasonably high levels of security and predictability to concentrate and do their best work. Other people are, or have learned to be, risk takers. Perhaps they were originally drawn to work in stable Fortune 500 companies but were later forced to learn to tolerate increasing levels of risk as the organization transformed itself. While some employees didn't make it and were let go or left voluntarily, the majority learned that basic change brings opportunities as well as losses, triumph as well as fear. A third group are the risk creators, people who flourish in conditions of high risk and swift change. To be fully alive, they need to be in situations where those conditions prevail.

In spite of the broad sweep of change in the macroeconomic sense, some nations, industries, and organizations are still essentially stable. They have seen relatively little change and any change that does occur happens slowly. These organizations offer considerable job security and honor seniority.

In the United States, these conditions are characteristic of colleges and universities, unionized organizations, and the core business of utilities and many governments. Relatively speaking, these are monopoly conditions. As such, they are fairly risk-free environments that have been only slightly affected by information technology and a borderless economy. People who are drawn to these conditions are motivated by security and predictability.

Low-risk organizations don't see time as money. They prefer to make decisions slowly and cautiously. The structure is usually hierarchical; employees are good soldiers who expect to be told what to do and how to do it. Although people are superficially polite face to face, they are basically competitive with each other as they vie for promotions and power. "Teamwork" and "empowerment" tend to be slogans rather than behaviors.

Most of the large and mature businesses in the United States have undergone major transformations in the past 25 years to become much faster, more innovative, and more productive. In response to greatly heightened global competition, these organizations have introduced much greater levels of risk.

People already working in those organizations had to learn how to step up to risk and deal with it—or leave. New hires are usually practiced risk takers.

Risk creators, those who thrive on risk and actively seek it out, tend to gravitate to one of two specific types of organizations: start-ups, which never have enough money or customers in the early years, and turn-arounds, which may have been successful in the past but aren't now. Both types are characterized by extremely high levels of risk along with potentially high payoffs. People who enjoy working in start-ups and turn-arounds are bored by security and predictability.

RISK AND CORPORATE CULTURE: DIGGING DEEPER

In part because of the differences in their structures and culture, high-risk organizations (usually flat meritocracies) and low-risk organizations (usually hierarchical and bureaucratic) are very different in many ways, including

- the kinds of experiences they offer
- their priorities and values
- amount and kinds of compensation
- opportunities for becoming a leader, being innovative, and making a difference

People who flourish in one will not flourish in the other. Low-risk organizations expect certain kinds of behaviors; those very behaviors are barriers to success in high-risk organizations, where fast experimentation and innovation are critical to beating the competition.

High-risk organizations are always under tremendous pressure to get much better results much faster using less money. In these intense organizations, nothing is wasted: not time or talent or knowledge. As a result, sharing resources and information is a given, and employees are colleagues who collaborate because the wolf is never far from the door. The organizational structure is relatively flat, and leadership flows from knowledge as well as job status. People of any age and at any level who have expertise are expected to initiate and use their judgment.

Many who join high-risk organizations prefer a work-dominated life in which they can innovate and lead. Some want the opportunity to make a lot of money and a chance to work on the next big breakthrough. Some want to build a successful organization, but many prefer to be individual contributors rather than climb the management ladder. Lots of these people are natural leaders in challenging conditions. My husband was the captain of Coast Guard ships for 15 years, and he loved to say, always with a big grin, "There's nothing like a great storm at sea when you have a good ship under you."

By contrast, in low-risk organizations time is truly not money. My hometown of San Diego has been studying possible locations for a new airport for about 50 years and has just conducted its 27th inconclusive multimillion-dollar study. Low-risk organizations tend to change very slowly and often only because there's a crisis. While absolute job security has become rare, these organizations come close. They tend not to lay people off, and they expect people to work only 35 to 40 hours a week. Leaders talk about empowering subordinates but in reality they issue orders. Subordinate input is discouraged or ignored and subordinates accept that. Since change is slow and there may not be much of it, experience is considered very important. People's ambition is usually tied to the next promotion and very few employees imagine more than one or two promotions.

Low-risk organizations offer more job security than high-risk or transformational organizations, and they attract, retain, and garner real loyalty from people for whom security is the highest priority.

It's important not to judge these organizations and the people who flourish in them. Some people like to know their place, like to know exactly what to do, and some prefer being pretty invisible. They would be comfortable in organizations that are naturally low risk. People who thrive in high-risk conditions are generally the reverse. They're not interested in hierarchical status; they prefer being autonomous, and they want to achieve visibility on the basis of a breakthrough accomplishment.

The key is to find a good match. Employees need to be clear on their comfort level with risk. Would they choose to work 60 to 80 hours a week and go for the brass ring, or would they rather have reasonable hours and a flexible work arrangement? Would they need to work in an organization with a no-layoff policy or would they prefer to join a start-up that's racing toward an initial public offering?

ASKING THE RIGHT QUESTIONS

When it comes to company policies and practices, one size no longer fits all. It's more appropriate to think in terms of Best Fit—a match between an individual's values, attitudes, and priorities and those of an organization—rather than in terms of Best Companies or Best Practices.

Organizations need to think through their values and culture:

- What do you expect from people?
- What are the personal qualities of most people who succeed in your organization?
- Which personal qualities easily earn respect and which lead to people becoming isolated?
- How liberal or conservative are your employees?

Here is an illustration. Jeff Koertzen had worked as a Human Resources manager for Microsoft for a long time, but he quit when Microsoft stopped supporting gay rights legislation in the state of Washington. Many of his coworkers were also disappointed; these techies were also idealists who believed that Microsoft was a special company because it stood for progressive values. A total of 1,741 Microsoft employees signed a petition asking the company to support the antidiscrimination bill; only 197 employees asked Microsoft to remain neutral. Chairman Bill Gates and CEO Steven Ballmer responded to the pressure and announced they would support the bill when it came up in the next legislative session.[2]

For their part, employees and prospective employees need to think through what they value and need.

- What are your priorities in the short and longer term?
- How available, accessible, and interruptible does the organization expect its employees to be?
- How available, accessible, and interruptible are current or prospective employees willing or able to be at this time?
- How much flexibility does the organization have in regard to when and where work is done?
- How much flexibility in regard to time and place do you prefer or require now?
- Is that likely to change in five years?
- How risky is the organization's future?
- Is the organization in an unusually competitive industry or slot?
- Does the organization routinely lay off people when margins are falling?
- Does the organization routinely retrain people when it enters or exits new businesses?
- Is off-shoring a vital and expanding part of the organization's profit strategy?
- How much and what kinds of risk are you comfortable with? In the past, did you seek risk by changing jobs or specialties or starting major new projects? Or did you do the opposite?
- How important is job security?

Individuals and organizations need to become clear about what they value, require, and prefer in terms of working conditions to make good choices. To facilitate the process of making things clear, I've constructed two questionnaires, one about the

Table 9.1
Analyzing the Organization

This Organization Is:
(Score 1 to 3) 1 = not very, 2 = pretty much, 3 = very much

Characteristic	Score	
	Today	In 2 years
Calm and deliberate		
Fast and decisive		
Very high risk		
Low-to-medium risk		
Entrepreneurial		
Slow; people wait for orders.		
Characterized by forthright challenges		
Filled with an intense hum		
Filled with people who think like employees		
Dominated by seniority		
Only results count		
Filled with high-risk/high-return excitement		
Quiet and comfortable, with few surprises		
Focused on business outcomes		
Dominated by staff and professionals		
Internally competitive		
Characterized by collegial relationships		

Characteristic	Score	
	Today	In 2 years
Results outweigh status		
Status outweighs results		
People tolerate boring work		
Learning and challenge are ongoing		
Exceeding personal expectations is vital		
Achieving success is immensely important		
People don't play together		
Having fun with colleagues is valued		
Individualism is a core value		
People expect everyone to be treated the same regardless of contribution		
People are polite and not forthcoming		
Loyalty is expected		
Wants employees to feel they're part of a family		
Competition is hidden		
Is changing rapidly in basic ways		
Expects to hear the truth		
Welcomes input from anyone with ideas and knowledge		
Assumes work comes first		
Expects people to be superheroes		

Table 9.2
Analyzing the Person

I want:
(Score 1 to 3) 1 = not very, 2 = pretty much, 3 = very much

My work assignments customized	
More flexible work arrangements	
Reasonable work hours	
Choice about benefits	
Choice about forms of compensation	
Opportunities to work on my ideas	
Options and a chance to get rich	
More autonomy	
Opportunities to make decisions and lead	
Work to be an exciting place	
Very clear goals	
Training/education	
Predictability and some job security	
The latest tools	
To work with the smartest people	
Fun colleagues	
To do important, cutting-edge work	
Opportunities to initiate	
Freedom to innovate	
A clear distinction between work and personal time	
An organization whose values fit with mine	

characteristics of an organization and another about what is important to an individual employee.[3] Smart individuals and astute organizations will make sure the majority of the priorities intersect like the teeth of a zipper.

Success is much more likely when there's a real compatibility between what the organization requires and the employee desires. Best Fit leads to high motivation and a sense of belonging. Bad Fit results in discomfort, high stress, and failure. Without Best Fit, the chances for success and retention plummet; with Best Fit, the chances for success soar.

CHAPTER TEN

STAYING AHEAD
OF THE CURVE

OVER THE YEARS, I have talked with several hundred organizational leaders about what they need to do to stay ahead of the competition. It always comes down to just one thing: the need for ever-increasing innovation and productivity. And how does an organization foster innovation? By supporting the fundamental qualities this book has been describing: trust and respect between employees and management that lead to mutual commitment and mutual goals. Those are the essential conditions for genuine collaboration, a feeling of "us."

Real teamwork uses the knowledge, creativity, and skills of everyone involved. Without that, continuous improvement and episodic breakthroughs are pipe dreams. With it, anything is possible.

This chapter offers a real-world example of the conditions and processes necessary for ever-increasing performance. Stephen

R. Hardis, former CEO of Cleveland's Eaton Corporation, a premier manufacturer of electrical components, fluid power equipment, and truck and automotive components, walked that road with stunning success. He was directly involved with Eaton's well-known transformations during the years he was executive vice-president and CEO, and here he shares his experiences.[1]

JB: I am very interested in hearing how the Eaton Corporation evolved from a traditional, very hierarchical, top-down organization to . . . well, I don't want to put words into your mouth.

SH: The big change came in 1968 . . .

JB: Give me the history from the end of World War II.

SH: Eaton began in 1910 making truck axles, and then before the war converted to engine components. After the war Eaton was a manufacturer of auto components and was 93 percent United Auto Workers union.

In 1968 the assumption was the plants were going to be unionized, and the principal strategy was to try to get a local union boss that Eaton management could work with. That year they opened a plant in Kearney, Nebraska, to make engine valves. Somewhere within the Eaton organization someone had read an article about a different industrial philosophy and the decision was made to experiment with it in Kearney.

While they had initially planned to bring in a union, they took the radical step of saying, "Let's try it without the union." When the plant first started, they put in practices that are now pretty commonplace but then were very unique. There was a lot of employee participation and the people in Kearney didn't have to clock in. There was no assigned parking for managers—which is basically a symbolic reference, but it sent an important and clear message.

Kearney started out with the idea that if you treat your employees as peers, you get their input. What was stunning to Eaton management was not only did the employees decide not to join the union, but the productivity of the plant was extraordinarily high. And this became a model for every Eaton plant since then—no Eaton plant in the United States has been unionized since '68 and about ten have decertified. Over time the "new Eaton philosophy" developed and it was very successful.

Then, in the early '80s Eaton went into crisis. It was the same pattern as a lot of U.S. industrial companies, but for us it happened earlier than most. Eaton responded by shutting about 20 plants, moving out of an entire segment of the business, and cutting employment from 63,000 at the peak to 36,000 at the trough.

When we came out of the recession in '83–84, then-Chairman Del DeWindt was very concerned that the whole Eaton philosophy had been ruptured by these actions, and there was a lot of internal discussion about how we could reinforce it. We assigned the task of figuring that out to a group of managers, and what came out of their discussion was the interesting insight that the model that had worked so well from '68 to the early '80s now felt a little paternalistic. It was not really a philosophy that emphasized mutual responsibility and mutual benefit.

So, in the '80s Eaton spent several years redefining the Eaton philosophy and then we spent several years communicating the new values.

The new perspective was that instead of Eaton being a very enlightened employer and a very good place for people to work, it was now an organization based on a set of values that embraced the idea of team. In Eaton's more advanced plants there are no foremen; the work is organized by teams. Stores are not locked up; they are kept in bins close to the workplace. Each work group interviews new hires, and they cross-train and divide the work among themselves. They figure out how to time the work through the plant. Interestingly, the workers took ownership of the process and that led to a marked improvement in quality. When this was implemented in the '90s, this was leading edge in the U.S. and it led to new levels of productivity.

One of the hidden costs of U.S. production was that using the traditional methods, you made the stuff, you inspected it, and if something was wrong you sent it back, it was reworked, the customer would inspect it and when he got it, if there was a flaw he would send it back. The understanding was the stuff was made, shipped to the customer's line, and installed in the product. If there was a defect it wasn't really caught until the final inspection of the finished good and then Eaton was responsible for the entire cost of redoing the product. Now customers were insisting on quality because they wanted to cut down on their cost of inspection and all of this created a tremendous emphasis on improving quality.

JB: What do you do with nonperformers? Does peer pressure control that?

SH: On the shop floor it's peer pressure. It's striking to me, if you have a team, if someone doesn't show up, doesn't carry their workload, or the quality is bad, the team will pressure to get rid of them. Among the knowledge workers, Eaton has gotten increasingly sophisticated about identifying the performers that aren't measuring up. You start out by making sure your raises and bonuses and promotions go to your better people and then you just have to start pruning the people. I found that your good people really resent it if you are not demanding enough of everybody.

We found that when everybody knew the product wasn't going to be inspected until it was delivered to the customer, everyone took ownership for quality and that led to material cost savings. This laid the groundwork for 6-sigma concepts which, within Eaton, are really driven by the workers. If you go on the shop floor the people you meet will be the team leaders, and they tell you what they need in order to improve productivity. They often come up with recommendations to change the tooling or for capital investments to save money.

To me, the conceptual breakthrough that Eaton made is the understanding that the real enemy is not the bosses but the overseas competition with people who are working for very low wages trying to take the work out of our plant. Personally, I don't think unions in general understand this; they perpetuate the traditional images of management versus employees, a sort of "us" always versus "them."

In that sense Eaton management and employees have values that are truly shared: everyone has a stake in winning, and the employees understand and embrace the idea that the way to protect your job is to give the customer a high-quality product at a competitive price. The responsibility for the design of the product is still essentially knowledge workers; the responsibility for marketing is still very much knowledge workers; but the responsibility for productivity and quality is very much the workers. Our best salesmen to the customers are the people on the shop floor. Nowadays customers are not doing a final inspection; they visit and they have people all over the plant to make sure that the methods we use are what they have approved. Customers don't want surprises, and they don't want recalls.

That really is the story of Eaton's transformation: from '68 to the early '80s was one revolution and the second started in the mid-'80s and it's still continuing. Eaton is driving lean concepts now, 6-sigma concepts, black belt concepts—

JB: What's black belt?

SH: Black belt is really an extension of 6-sigma. You train a group of people with sophisticated techniques for identifying the areas in which there are systemic problems and give them the tools to solve them, which again leads to improved quality and improved productivity.

One of the real benefits that none of us anticipated was that by changing the flow of work away from traditional banks of machines to a more logical flow, closing the storerooms and putting the goods next to the workers, shipping almost daily to the customers when they want products, all of a sudden we realized that we had freed up a huge amount of plant space, which was an unexpected dividend. Because of that space we could bid on additional business without building a new plant. One of the insights that really was pioneered by the Japanese was that you don't optimize equipment usage, you optimize inventory turns. If you don't have to build plant space and you are optimizing inventory turns, it's worth it to invest in more equipment because you really can become more competitive if you're shipping in just hours to the end customer.

So Eaton began to pick up market share and fill the plant with more equipment. Even though the equipment and the methods were more productive, jobs in Eaton plants were more secure than in the unionized plants, which weren't as competitive and were really becoming factories of last resort.

JB: When you say unionized plants, is that unionized within Eaton or your competition?

SH: Our competition. The bulk of Eaton is nonunion; we've acquired some companies with unions but there is no Eaton product in which a union can shut down production. If we've got a union plant that went on strike, there are other plants that are tooled to make the same product. I literally can't remember the last time there was a strike in any of Eaton's remaining unionized plants.

JB: I think you told me there are only two.

SH: There are only two UAW; there are some Machinist union, there are some Electrical Workers. But one of the things that happened is if the union really obstructed the ability to bring in new manufacturing techniques and productivity equipment in the traditional union plants that we acquired, those were the plants that were shut, particularly because we didn't need the floor-space capacity. I know of no products in Eaton which can be threatened by overseas competitors because of lower labor rates.

JB: That's astonishing!

SH: The Chinese Miracle is a failure of U.S. management. Eaton is more profitable than ever. Productivity is high, and we have differentiated products. One of the big advantages is that Eaton plants are located globally. If you are going to optimize inventory and your costs, you really can't put a plant in the middle of China to take advantage of low labor rates and then have to transport it to a ship, freight it over, and then bring it to a plant. The cost of that inventory and the costs associated with long lead times are so high, when a customer changes his schedule it means that inevitably you are going to have either excess inventory or you are going to run short, which means you are going to have to air freight product so that the plant doesn't shut down. On a global basis the Eaton model is much more competitive. We no longer have excess capacity on a geographic basis, which was a large hidden cost that we felt you had to have because you can't afford to shut down your customer. We can take advantage of a global supply chain without shutting our North American or European plants.

Eaton also got very good at knowing when it's best to out-source commodity products, like castings, forgings, some of your machine parts, because those essentially are products that can be made less expensively. Then, in some cases because of steel quotas, you can buy steel less expensively overseas, machine it, forge it, cast it, and bring it over as a part. So the Eaton strategy is to use its capital for those manufacturing practices which are reasonably distinctive and which allow them to be as close as possible to the customer. The result is we are not as vertically integrated as we were 20 years ago.

It is true that within North America the plants have gravitated to some of the border states in the South, Mexico, and the Caribbean for tax reasons. In Europe, the jobs have moved progressively to Eastern Europe because the shipping isn't hard and the workforce behind the Iron Curtain is incredibly well educated. But you don't have to bring it in from China or Malaysia because of the quality of the European or North American workforce.

JB: Do Eaton employees have a considerable amount of job security?

SH: It varies according to the line of work. In some businesses where there's a very cyclical aspect to the end market, like the heavy-duty truck market, they will go through periodic downturns. Because Eaton has very generous traditional defined benefit pension and postretirement medical benefits, we find the workers come back, and we don't have to retrain them. Over the course of their career they are very well paid. If we have to have layoffs, workers will often get together and discuss what's the best way to do it. Some of the older people will take unpaid vacations and they may split out the work.

There's a great deal of transparency. If you go into a plant you'll see all sorts of charts of productivity, all sorts of charts of incoming orders, all sorts of charts of the profitability of that plant, all sorts of data about their competitors, so if there is a downturn the workers aren't surprised, and there's a lot of discussion between them and management. Eaton workers understand we can't afford to have people not working—the customer won't pay for it. Which gives us a great advantage over a UAW unionized plant where workers go into a job bank when they're not needed, and they have to be paid when they do no work. That makes productivity gains almost pointless.

JB: And they don't do *any* work?

SH: They don't do any work if there is a job bank. Our people are generally among the higher paid in total compensation in the area in which they work. They don't make as much as a UAW worker in Detroit, but they also understand that their future is a lot more certain because Eaton is very competitive.

JB: Do the people in the plant participate in decisions beyond those of their particular work?

SH: It depends on the plant and the plant manager. A good plant manager will discuss everything with the workers, from the new products coming—

JB: So, it's an open book?

SH: Yes, in some of the older plants it may be limited to a particular department they work in, but the model is "we're in this together." I used to go to plants, and the people on the floor would talk to me about the fact that someone was coming from a customer because we were bidding on a large contract. They knew the product, they knew the contract, they knew who we were bidding against, and they knew that when the person showed up that it was important to be able to be part of the selling process.

JB: Does Eaton offer education, updating skills?

SH: Yes, Eaton has embraced the idea of continuous learning and has mandated that everybody has so many hours of training. Since I've retired, they've opened a training center in Cleveland and bring people in; they do a lot of online training. They've gotten very far in online job posting, and if people are interested they can see the job description and they can see what skills are required. Eaton has very generous tuition reimbursement programs. So people who are trying to get ahead can do that either through Eaton training or a lot of times there will be a relationship with a local community college, and the plant and the college will design courses specifically tailored to some of the more sophisticated requirements we have to allow people to move ahead. Yes, there is a tremendous investment in training. In talking to people today, I find they are always coming from one training program or another.

JB: So, Eaton takes the welfare of its employees unusually seriously.

SH: I really believe that's true. One of the great strengths of Eaton that we saw in the early '80s when we went through this tremendous restructuring was that our trained people whom we wanted to stay came back to work for us, and there was a genuine realization on the part of management that the sense of commitment to the company was one of our great competitive advantages. And then it became increasingly evident that in a time when you can't promise people total job security, we had to work hard to maintain a level of mutual trust to maintain that competitive advantage.

I'm proud of the fact that Eaton still has defined benefit pension plans. We know that some of the younger knowledge workers would much prefer defined contributions and cash balances that are portable, and in some of the higher-tech Eaton plants there are different programs. It is also critically important that Eaton has a very good healthcare system. As part of the social contract, we take care of our people, and they take care of their families. At least when I was still at Eaton health care was tailored so a single working mother could insure her kids and wouldn't opt out because she couldn't afford it.

Some of your senior, better-paid people had more aggressive demands and one of the things in terms of the fringe benefits that has become increasingly true is we need to give people choices, recognizing that single workers have different problems than somebody who has a family with young children. And when the kids are no longer eligible for health benefits, their parents have different requirements, and people have different preferences.

JB: Yes, in this book I'm calling that "customize." Create a cafeteria of choices in line with your organization's values and let people select what they most need or want *at this time.*

SH: A hidden benefit of computers is it used to be said we couldn't offer choices, and all of a sudden computers made it very easy to have a lot more flexibility. That's a great thing.

JB: One of the variables that has become very important is more people are really pressuring for a better work and family balance. Does Eaton get involved with that?

SH: You have to make a distinction within Eaton between knowledge workers and touch labor. If you take the people in the plant doing touch labor, they are much less concerned about the quality of their work experience in psychological terms. They're concerned mostly about their security, compensation, and their postretirement benefits. They want the workplace to be safe and increasingly our plants are air-conditioned for their comfort.

Knowledge workers have a different attitude and expectations. In a lot of cases you are talking about couples, married or unmarried, where both are working, and you have to satisfy the requirements of both. It's understood that if you can't give people with great potential the opportunity to be intellectually challenged so they're enhancing their skills and work is fun, you probably can't retain them. Knowledge workers just have very different values than the traditional people in the plant. They are probably very interested in what the share purchase plan will offer them and will they get capital appreciation, and they are more mobile and much more concerned about where they live.

For example, Eaton's plants are typically in very small towns, normally without commercial air transportation. In downturn times, people often go back to the farm. But in managing knowledge workers you have to locate in areas where both members of a couple can pursue their career and they can have the quality of life they want in terms of education, culture, and weather. You can no longer just locate your knowledge workers next to your plant. You can solve some of these issues through electronic communication and by corporate jets that go back and forth between where the knowledge workers are and the plant. This is a revolutionary change.

JB: What you described in the plant is a high level of collaboration between the hands-on people and management. Now, when you are talking about knowledge workers who have very different requirements, is that kind of a dividing line in Eaton?

SH: I think there is a potential for one. One of the things that probably mitigates it is, if you go to an Eaton plant today, there is a minimum of office people supervising the plant people so you don't have that friction. And you will find knowledge workers on the floor helping figure out how to manufacture the product and solving some of the quality problems. So there's a level of interaction where people are working together. But, I do think as you think ahead that with knowledge workers having different educational backgrounds and living in different locations, that's a fault line that can get worse.

My own feeling is that within Eaton there was a sense of esprit and loyalty to the company that bridged that line. One of the things that probably helps diffuse the potential problem is the knowledge workers who choose to work at Eaton—it's a self-selecting process—are people who like to work as part of a team, and they often like to be part of a group that makes something.

They are not the same sort of people who would be in New York in a hedge fund or on the West Coast doing entertainment types of jobs.

As the knowledge work gets so much more educated and specialized and rarified, we may not be able to attract sophisticated knowledge workers to an Eaton. We may find we have to draw on people who really think of themselves as IT specialists or other forms of specialist who don't think of themselves as Eaton people. While it hasn't emerged yet, I think that is a potential problem.

JB: There are probably six key things that people want now, and one of them is some reasonable amount of security. As the direction is toward less job security, it is reasonable that employees' commitment to an Eaton which offers significant commitment to them will increase.

SH: Right now the direction overall is toward less job security, so it's reasonable to think that Eaton employees will feel increased commitment toward a company that demonstrates significant commitment toward them.

One of the things that Eaton has going for it—and most people who are in corporate life will cynically dismiss it—is most of our people are very proud to say they work for Eaton.

JB: When people say "I'm with Eaton," that is really a sign of identification with the company.

SH: I found that Eaton people were very proud when their plant managers were heading the United Way or they were senior civic leaders. I think that people badly underestimate the desire of people to be associated with an organization that makes them feel proud. You know, it may sound like a *non sequitur,* but MBNA, the largest independent credit card issuer in the world, developed a whole credit card edge with affinity cards because people really wanted some identification with something they took pride in, in a world in which they felt anonymous. Eaton people have great pride in the company. They say, "I work for Eaton," and they love it when the stock price goes up even though they may not own a lot of shares, because it means we are winning. They love it when Eaton introduces a new product, they love it when Eaton wins, and one of the things that Eaton has to continue to work hard at is making sure that everybody in Eaton is given credit because when everybody on the team receives psychological credit they buy into that credit.

JB: Do you have many people who only work for Eaton for their whole career?

SH: Yes, still. It's not so much true of the knowledge workers, but even among the knowledge workers our turnover is so low that at times the Human Resource people have said we don't have enough turnover to assure we are bringing in some other skills or new skills. Our retention level, even with periodic cyclical downturns, is very high. And, yes, people at Eaton still think of this as a career although in some cases it hasn't proven to be correct, but they still do. And so the contemporary model where everybody is moving on just doesn't apply to Eaton and the Eatons of the world.

JB: Can you give me an example of Eaton employees' high levels of commitment and engagement?

SH: In the late '90s, when the automotive market was unexpectedly strong, and we picked up business we didn't expect to get, we had a real problem keeping up with the orders. It was a plant in Kearney, Nebraska, that worked on Ford engine valves, and they jumped in and worked three shifts seven days a week, except for Christmas and New Year's Day, for almost an entire year. What the workers did was figure out ways office people could come in to spell the people on the floor, in the summer some of the kids would come home from college and work, and on a few occasions some retired people came back to work. People that weren't part of this culture would say, "Well, what did you pay them to do that?," and the fact is that would have been insulting. They were paid, and they obviously got overtime, and the plant is a very good plant, but the workers wanted . . . well, when I visited the plant the next spring to thank them, what they basically wanted to know was, Do you understand what we did, the sacrifice, and what are you going to do so the next time the market turns up we don't have to go through that process because this isn't the way we want to live. The workers didn't feel abused because it was understood that we were winning, we were getting business, we were taking customers orders. That year we had so few rejects it's almost statistically impossible to find them—which the customers loved.

As soon as we could, we invested in additional capacity so it wouldn't happen again. That's the kind of social contract that has to exist between the enterprise and the individual. I literally asked what is it we can do to thank you, and one woman stood up and said, "Give me some time off" and everybody laughed and then she said, "But not if it means we are not going to meet the customer's requirements." And I thought that said it all.

JB: Absolutely, and what happened?

SH: Oh, we met all requirements, we picked up market share, and we increased capacity, we put some equipment in there, we off-loaded some of the slow-moving items to other plants so that these people could concentrate.

The other experience I remember vividly was we took a group of workers from a plant in Iowa to New York in order to introduce them at the annual meeting with security analysts. They were a group of young men, some of whom were high-school stars—they weren't college graduates—and they had won the competition for better ideas.

We didn't think that security analysts had any idea how you really make a plant more competitive, so they weren't giving us credit for the fact that we were truly more competitive than our competition. So this group of workers came to New York and made a presentation on what their team did. A few cynical New York sell-side analysts quizzed them incredulously like they were idiots, and one guy said, "And what do you get out of this?" I distinctly remember this one young man looked him in the eye and said, "I get to keep my job." And there was total silence and nobody else asked a nasty question. It was great.

JB: That was terrific!

SH: Yeah, that was the answer. They understood this wasn't an adversarial process. Their plant was winning—they got to keep their job in the town of Belmond, Iowa, and working for Eaton was a preferred place to work. They weren't going to be making engine valves in China; they were making engine valves in Iowa, close to the customer. And with that kind of attitude you can win.

JB: And it's sustained?

SH: Well, if you look at the track record in the last five years since I retired, Eaton continues to have record results. They continue to outgrow their own markets, which is ultimately the test of whether you are successful; and because Eaton is more productive and its profits are good and its balance sheet is strong, Eaton can afford to invest more in product development, in training, in mass marketing. We can afford to invest more to go into global markets.

If you open a plant in an overseas country, people on the outside tend to say, "Oh, my god, the giant sucking sound is that of work leaving the States." The fact is that if you take shipments of key components and supplies, you increase the total size of the pie. It's not just a case of dividing the static pie. I'm always frustrated by observers who think of it as a static pie. The trick is to make the pie bigger so everybody can win, and that's something that people have got to understand that we are able to do. And the company has to keep faith with the people and make the investments in product differentiation. They've got to make the investments in capital equipment and advanced tooling.

Again, one of the anecdotes I always remember is we bought a circuit-breaker plant in China and when I toured the plant, I told the plant manager we had to put in safety equipment. He was insulted—he thought I was insulting the plant. It took me a while to say every Eaton plant, regardless of where it is, has the same safety equipment, the same environmental equipment, because we are committed to our people. It's not a question of what the laws are. All we are doing is bringing it up to Eaton's standards because we don't like people putting their hands in the punch press where they could get hurt. And that's the way Eaton does it.

I finally convinced him that I wasn't putting him, or the plant, down; this was Eaton's standards. Well, people understand that. They do understand when they see the company making those investments. They understand that the company is making investments in environmental stuff before they are required to. It's part of building the sense of esprit, of pride of being Eaton.

JB: Yes, and it sounds like you do a heck of a job in getting people engaged.

SH: One of the things that used to strike me was that people in Eaton plants wear a lot of Eaton logo clothing.

JB: That's very interesting!

SH: Sometimes we give those items as a thank you if you do something exceptional. But there is enough demand so there is a catalog and they go online to buy it! That's their identification; they are proud to wear an Eaton T-shirt, jacket, or cap. They are proud of that; and the individual Eaton plant will have their own stuff and almost invariably if I left a plant they would give me a sweatshirt or a cap from their plant. They wanted me to wear it when I walked around their plant and I took it very seriously because, to them, it was a really important thing.

JB: Because of a sense of commitment . . . community . . .

SH: It was commitment, a sense of identity, of pride. . . . I said when I retired, as long as our people are proud to work for Eaton the future is assured. Nobody knows what's going to happen in technologies or competition. But if people continue to have pride in working at Eaton, I was confident of the future. We'd find a solution to everything else.

JB: So the transformation from the classic adversarial union-management, worker-management rift starts with an idea in Kearney, Nebraska, in 1968, because someone said let's try doing it differently, and success flowed from soliciting input in areas in which people were truly expert—whatever their status.

SH: The key to it is you have to genuinely believe that that's your source of competitive advantage. The managements that understand this is the competitive advantage and treat that as a core value, almost as a form of industrial religion, will win. The people who adopt it because they think it's a good technique to keep out the union, that will be self-defeating. We didn't see this as union busting. We saw it as a way of beating the competition, getting more business, and genuinely enlisting the help of our people. And the people in Eaton who didn't get it, had no future within the company.

One thing that used to annoy me enormously is people who make artificial divisions between tech businesses and traditional businesses, knowledge-worker jobs and worker jobs. The fact is every business today incorporates an incredible amount of sophisticated technology, or a sophisticated understanding of global markets, and the ability to use information technology techniques and understand 6-sigma. So while Eaton people might have different personalities, maybe different experience, different skill base, different motivation, the level of intelligence in an Eaton location is at least as high as might be found on a campus or in an investment bank.

But what I find is that people who have never worked in corporate life, really don't believe in the marketplace, they don't trust worker involvement. They really believe that a bunch of very well-educated, bright people should come up with a solution to save these poor people. They can't get beyond their own lack of experience and erroneous perceptions. Over and over again I met people like that who just don't understand. They hadn't been part of it, they hadn't walked the floor, they hadn't talked to people who had been part of it, and so they were cynical. They really don't understand that the market is going to weed out the people that abuse their workers. The market really does work, it does work.

CHAPTER ELEVEN

HOW ARE WE DOING ECONOMICALLY?

U P UNTIL NOW, this book has focused on issues that are crucially important to individual people and organizations. In this and the next two chapters, the view expands to the nation as a whole. The gravity of these issues also speaks to the future of many countries, including, especially, the United States.

For those who would understand the larger issues, the first rule comes from the first page of the textbook for my long-ago class in Introduction to Statistics: *"Remember, figures don't lie, but liars figure."* The second rule follows from the first: *"Don't believe everything you read . . . or hear."*

How are we doing economically? The answer depends in large part on who answers the question. Consider the following bits of economic news and analysis. A few of them were published in 2005 but the great majority come from 2006. It would seem that a large committee of blindfolded people drew very different conclusions from patting down our elephantlike economy.

- Many people can't believe the economy is booming because they haven't experienced any gains. In fact most families—those in the middle of the income pack—lost ground.[1] That has happened five years in a row. Making things worse, the number of people without health insurance has risen.
- The U.S. unemployment rate remained a low 4.6 percent in June 2006, the average time it takes people to find a new job is less than six weeks, and pay increased 4.6 percent in the second quarter of 2006.[2] Profits and productivity have continued to rise, and in today's current tight labor market, wages should continue to increase.
- While the Gross Domestic Product continues its five years of strong growth, workers' compensation—wages and benefits—only increased 2.4 percent in the first quarter of 2006.[3] As inflation rose by 3.4 percent in the year that ended in March 2005, compensation is not even keeping up with increasing prices. In 2004 the Labor Department found that 51.6 percent of all workers were in five job categories with average pay of $15.50 an hour. These employees are the ones who are most likely to feel pain as gasoline prices and credit rates rise.
- Wages and benefits rose in the first quarter of 2006 by nine percent and in the second quarter of 2006 by 4.9 percent.[4] Workers with specialized skills in areas of labor shortages are most likely to be receiving compensation increases.
- Unemployment, economic growth, and inflation have been very good in the American economy over the past quarter century.[5] But we also have falling individual savings rates and increasing debt, as well as rising trade and budget debts. The wage gap—more properly thought of as a wealth gap—is increasing, headed, most visibly, by shocking CEO compensation.
- The economy is continuing to grow despite slowdowns in the automobile and housing industries.[6] The unemployment rate

in November 2006 was slightly less than 4.5 percent. Average hourly pay in November was 4.1 percent higher than a year ago. The compensation of newly hired skilled or management people had increased from eight to ten percent over the previous year.

- In September 2006, the World Economic Forum released its international competitive rankings and continued to downgrade the United States into sixth place because its budget is not balanced, it has major unlimited costs in defense and homeland security, and it has a low national savings rate and a high trade deficit.[7] (The WEF ignored the facts of very low unemployment, high productivity gains, and a budget deficit that is approaching only two percent of GDP.)
- Despite continued volatility, or "rolling recessions" like the ones we have now in autos and housing, the number of recessions and their severity have declined.[8] From 1970 to 1982, we had four recessions that lasted a total of four years, and unemployment climbed as high as 10.8 percent. From 1982 to 2006, we've experienced two recessions that lasted a total of one year and four months, with unemployment peaking at 7.8 percent.
- At 62 percent in 2005, America has among the highest rates of employment in the world. But while the economy has grown by almost 12 percent since the recession of 2001, *median* household income declined by 0.5 percent.[9]
- While there is high job turnover in certain specialties and firms, national job stability patterns are not much different from the 1970s and 1980s. Male workers older than 45 are about as likely to work for an employer for 20 years as they were in 1969.[10]
- Much of the seeming increase in high incomes has been the result of "tax shifting," moving from filing as a business to filing as an individual when individual tax rates were lowered.[11] This switch did not make the rich richer but it did exaggerate the apparent increase in the top one percent's share of income, which was 7.2 percent in 1988 and also 7.2 percent

from 2002 to 2004. The claim that there has been a dramatic increase in income inequality in the past 20 years is not true. There is no trend after 1988 in the inequality of distribution of disposable income, wages, consumption, or wealth.

- Biotech, a major industry in my home town of San Diego, has experienced a major shift in the past few years as increasing amounts of research are moving offshore to China, India, and Eastern Europe, where skills are high and wages are low.[12] The current fear is that job creation in the industry will be unable to keep up with job losses.

- The declining power of unions is evidenced not only by the small number of members but, more dramatically, by the small number of strikes.[13] The Bureau of Labor Statistics reports that 2.8 million workers went on 470 strikes in 1952. In 1994 there were 45 strikes involving 322,000 workers. In 2004, 171,000 workers walked out in 17 strikes.

- Most Americans and many nations are growing wealthier.[14] Our recovery has grown at roughly twice the rate of Europe and, in terms of corporate profits and productivity, we have had one of the most impressive growth cycles. The growth of jobs in financial services, medical technology, software design, and other growth industries is vastly larger than the loss of jobs in the automotive industries. By 2005, workers earned more than they did at the height of the 1990s growth period. But the largest increase in wealth came from rising values in homes and stock. The net worth of a median household is estimated at $100,000. While the rich are getting richer, so are the tens of millions of people in the middle class.

- American job growth and churn have been impressive since the last recession, but the wage gap increased with the top 20 percent of earners' income rising in 2005 by two percent after inflation while the income of the middle 20 percent grew by only 0.9 percent.[15] But wages *and* benefits have been roughly the same share of GDP for the last half century.[16]

- At the same time, for the 82 countries for which there were good data in 2004, real GDP had risen an average of 4.4 percent a year from 2000 to 2004 for an average total of 18.9 percent.[17] Big national winners included China, Korea, Lithuania, Romania, Ireland, Chile, New Zealand, Australia, South Africa, and Nigeria. The relative standing of countries changed very little—China was number 61 in 2000 and number 60 in 2004—because all the other countries were also growing.

By now the astute reader will have noticed that each positive example was followed by a negative one and the reverse. What can we learn from this?

Economics really is the dreary science, and when it's in bed with politics, it's a prostitute. In any large statistical analysis, there are enough numbers to create any selective case you want to "prove." In addition, the reader must be wary of words like "averages" because they often blur or hide exceptions. "Average wages," "average income," and "average hourly earnings" can lead to false conclusions. For example, average hourly earnings don't include benefits, tips, bonuses, or commissions. And, very basically, an economy of a nation—much less the worldwide economy—is so complex that it is very difficult to accurately assess how well or badly all of the parts are doing unless you're reviewing those outcomes several years or decades after the fact.

> Economics really is the dreary science, and when it's in bed with politics, it's a prostitute. In any large statistical analysis, there are enough numbers to create any selective case you want to "prove."

What are the facts? Who knows? And how much weight do they carry, anyway? Our viewpoints and thus our behaviors and choices are not primarily determined by objective facts. Instead, they are driven by how we perceive things through our partisan lenses. Make no mistake: whether it comes from what we read in the press or our personal experiences or tales we grew up with, we all have firm opinions and expectations. As a result, all of our lenses are colored by our very partisan views. So "How are we doing economically?" is not an easy question to answer objectively. But, overall, I think the American economy as a whole has demonstrated extraordinary resilience since 2001. Most of the statistics are significantly positive. But families and individuals may be faced with unexpected economic perils at any time.

WHY MANY PEOPLE
FEEL DEFENSELESS

There never has been a time when people thought the going was easy. The idyllic "golden days" are sugar coated by selective memory. But the going really has gotten harder in the last 15 years, and there will be no going back to a less stressful time because the ever-increasing competition arises out of basic structural changes like information technology.

The great economist Joseph Schumpeter described a phenomenon he called "creative destruction": the death of older, inefficient organizations and their replacement by new, vastly more productive ones. While creative destruction is very healthy for an economy as a whole, it can be disastrous for individuals, for it strips all vestiges of security from those who work in a particular organization or industry. And it is happening faster and faster these days, simply because there has been a phenomenal growth in the number of people and organizations participating in the global economy.

In addition, risk is being shifted from organizations to employees at an increasing pace. Two concrete examples are the changes in pensions and healthcare benefits. Even very large and prestigious corporations like IBM, Hewlett-Packard, and Verizon Communications have frozen at least some pensions. Typically, new employees are frozen out of the pension plan, while older workers are owed the benefits they've already earned but can no longer add to that fund.

> Risk is being shifted from organizations to employees at an increasing pace.

Defined benefit plans are giving way to 401(k) plans in which employees become responsible for managing their retirement funds. At the same time companies are increasingly offering "limited-benefit" health insurance plans that cover routine maintenance but not medical crises, while the companies simultaneously cut retirees' health benefits.

The auto industry's Big Three—General Motors, Ford, and Chrysler—are all in deep financial trouble because, with the exception of a few models, they have not been producing popular vehicles, even as they are saddled with huge retiree pension and healthcare obligations. In desperation, auto makers are offering older workers buyout packages that limit or even eliminate future retirement benefits in exchange for a one-time cash payout. In 2006 General Motors, alone, offered buyouts to more than 100,000 employees and 35,000 accepted. At about the same time, roughly 36,000 Ford employees chose the buyout incentive package. Early in December 2006 investor Kirk Kerkorian sold the last of his $1.2 billion in GM shares. Thus, a major investor and many thousands of employees voted their lack of confidence in their organization's future with their feet.

Institutions in which we ground our faith and on which we psychologically depend for all kinds of support are failing us. The Catholic Church, especially, is riddled with sexual scandals and is paying out compensation to sexually abused victims in the millions of dollars. The divorce rate continues to average about 50 percent a year, which means there are very few families that have not experienced the wrench of heartbreak and the breakup of the nuclear unit.

Major corporate scandals from Enron to WorldCom and reports of scandalous CEO salaries have left people with little faith in corporations. Corporate profits have soared but average wage increases have barely kept up with inflation. Healthcare and energy costs keep increasing. Eighty percent of the federal government's current budget deficits are for the unfunded entitlements of Social Security and Medicare, and no one is addressing the issue.[18] It's currently estimated that every American household owes $500,000 for all federal obligations for unfunded Congressional programs that Congress legislated but did not include in the federal budget.

Jobs of all types—high end as well as low end—are disappearing from the United States, moving to the millions of motivated, educated, and skilled foreign workers who are eager to work for fractions of the compensation Americans take for granted. And, with the exception of the civil service and teachers unions, unions have become weak. Their membership has fallen from 35.5 percent of the workforce in 1945 to 12.0 percent today, with only 7.9 percent in the private sector.[19]

What's the solution to this exodus of jobs and the loss of security? The suggestion we hear most often, as a cure for all our problems, is "more education." But is it really the panacea when so much of our educational system is broken?

Michael Bloomberg, the mayor of New York City, recently described our education establishment as being akin to the 1970s American automobile industry in which production was geared to the needs of the workers and not the customers.[20] The United States spends more than any other country on education, but the rate of return on this investment is wretched. Many of the problems that are identified as causes of the poor performance of American students K–12 are rationalizations for the failure of the system. Through most of the twentieth century, we had all those same problems—gangs, legal and illegal immigration, domestic turbulence, poverty, and wars—and yet the educational level of the American workforce was second to none.

> The suggestion we hear most often, as a cure for all our problems, is "more education." But is it really the panacea when so much of our educational system is broken?

Another idea often suggested as a solution to our loss of jobs is protectionism, which seeks to increase a nation's control of its own destiny and diminish the turbulence caused by creative destruction by closing its borders to external competitors.

Unfortunately, the major outcome of closing the borders through high tariffs and taxes is a major decline in trade and trade-related jobs. The 1929 depression began as an ordinary recession until our politicians effectively closed the borders to international trade.

Another form of protectionism makes it very expensive to fire or lay off employees. In those countries, there is very little job churn.

The churn—the loss or growth of jobs—in the American economy is enormous. In 2005, every month, on average, 4.5 million Americans either left their job of their own accord or they were laid off or fired; 4.8 million started a new job. It's not just a matter of outsourcing or insourcing any more. Increasingly we see churn within a company as it moves out of some businesses and into others. Hewlett-Packard, for example, has cut 30 percent of its employees worldwide since 2002, but its headcount has remained steady at 150,000.[21] Hewlett-Packard has become a nimble employer, hiring people with the right skills in promising parts of the business even as it had large layoffs of employees whose skills were no longer valuable and who were expensive to keep.

In contrast, in Western Europe and many other nations in which it is very expensive to let people go, there is almost no churn. But there is also no job growth. The stagnation resulting from rigid labor rules causes slow growth in the economy and very high long-term unemployment rates.[22]

Competition has increased everywhere, and no part of the globe is immune. Efforts to resist change and maintain the status quo, while understandable, are always short sighted. In February 2006, German municipalities set out to increase the work week from 38.5 hours to 40.[23] At the same time, France's Prime Minister Dominique de Villepin made it easier for small companies to hire and fire people, which resulted in the employment of 170,000 people who had been jobless. The response in both countries to these small changes was nationwide protests.

Rigid labor laws that seek to protect employees from today's realities often have draconian negative outcomes. When it is very expensive to fire people, employers don't hire and investors don't invest. When it is very expensive to downsize, employers choose bankruptcy before moving to a more accommodating country.[24] High severance costs, designed to offer protection to employees, cost the economy in every way, especially in terms of jobs.

THE PERCEPTION OF CHANGE IS GREATER THAN THE REALITY

There is a natural churn in the American economy that affects industries, not just jobs. Before national economies were part of a global network, industries in one country would slump when demand for their products declined and people would be laid off. Then later, as demand increased, people would be hired (or rehired), and jobs as well as the industry would recover. Changes in this pattern started in the 1980s when industries started sending jobs off-shore; the result was that even if the industry became profitable, the jobs did not return.

However, the perception of risk and change is far larger than the reality. The Federal Reserve Bank of New York found that 2.9 million jobs were outsourced overseas between 1997 and 2003.[25] That amounted to an average of 40,000 jobs lost each month or 2.4 percent of the total U.S. labor force in 2003. Balanced against that figure is the number of jobs the United States *gained* from work shifted from overseas to the United States. Since 1990, the

> The perception of risk and change is far larger than the reality.

number of jobs moved into the United States from overseas increased by 82 percent, a much higher figure than the 23 percent rise in jobs that were outsourced.[26] While there are no definitive reports of the number of jobs insourced to the United States, from 1991 to 2001, the number of jobs insourced increased from about 4.9 million in 1991 to roughly 6.4 million in 2001.

In March 2004, Dr. Ben Bernanke, then chairman of the economics department at Princeton and a governor of the Federal Reserve, and now chairman of the Fed, observed that in the past decade the U.S. economy had lost, on average, 15 million jobs a year from all causes.[27] He estimated that only about one percent of the 15 million jobs were lost to offshore facilities. At the same time, we created an average of 17 million new jobs a year. The amount of churn in the American economy is evidence of an extraordinary rate of creative destruction.

It is reasonable to conclude that, to date, the major indices of economic health do not reveal any significant impacts from either outsourcing or insourcing on the millions of jobs in the American economy.

Still, how are we doing? Many economists believe the best assessments of economic health are provided by the unemployment rate and the rate of labor compensation.

The current rate of unemployment is below five percent, which is historically very low. Some people criticize the unemployment figure as being unrealistically low because it ignores discouraged and underemployed people, but that is simply wrong. According to the Bureau of Labor, the rate of discouraged and underemployed workers has not increased compared with the mid-1990s.[28] The percentage of people in the labor force dipped from 67 percent in January 2001 to 66 percent in August 2004. That decline is mostly the result of the huge increase in unemployed teenagers (ages 16 to 19), from five percent in 2000 to 43 percent in 2004. The rest is composed of people who have chosen to go to school, or retire early, or stay home and take care of children.

In June 2006, four years into the recovery from the 2001 recession, there was an increase of almost 250,000 jobs, and wages for that quarter increased 4.6 percent, the largest increase since 1997.[29]

This recovery has been described as a poor second cousin to the one in the 1990s, especially in wage increases. But a new analysis by the Treasury Department found that wages fell by 1.5 percent in the first half (62 months) of the 1990s, while in the 62 months of this current economic expansion, wages increased by 0.7 percent.[30] The same study found that, after inflation, total compensation (wages and benefits) in this recovery gained 7.4 percent, compared with two percent in the 1990s expansion. (The largest compensation gain in the 1990s was in the second half of the decade.) In other words, larger increases in compensation have already begun and should continue as long as the economy is healthy, businesses are profitable, and the unemployment rate remains low.

Basically, the claims that wages and benefits are stagnant—or worse—and workers are doing really poorly compared with the 1990s is turning out to be wrong when the same measure of economic *averages* of the population, which includes wages and benefits, are compared. In 2006, the real average wage for workers increased by 2.8 percent, or about $1,200 per household. Although many companies are changing to 401(k)s from traditional pensions and most are passing along some of the rising cost of health insurance, fringe benefits have risen by 39 percent since 2000.

Despite a widely held belief that workers are losing ground, especially when compared with the 1990s, the pattern of wage increases in this recovery is basically the same as it was in the 1990s. Increases in wages always occur after the economy has started to grow and profits and productivity have risen. The large paycheck increases in the 1990s started in 1997, and they began in this recovery in 2006.

Another idea that never proved true concerns a change in the nature of work. During the 1990s, especially, pundits were predicting that people were moving into an era in which careers would no longer be based on long-term employment with a few employers. Instead, they said, life would be made up of six, or 10, or 15 different careers, marked by different employers, in different industries, using different skills and knowledge.

That change never materialized. The Labor Department's report of changes in average job tenure for mature male workers between 1983 and 2004 have been far more modest than that:[31]

Age	1983 Years with employer	2004 Years with employer
25–34	5.9	5.1
35–44	7.3	5.2
45–54	12.8	9.6

There is, though, a new trend. Data from 2005, when wages really started increasing in this recovery period, revealed the highest rate of job changes for employees of both sexes and all ages since 2000, which is when the U.S. government began collecting this information.[32] While headlines usually highlight big layoffs, in 2005 there were 364,000 more new hires a month, on average, than there were employee separations. In an increasingly healthy economy, every month millions of Americans change jobs, the great majority voluntarily as they seek opportunities with greater responsibility, higher pay, or both.

The strong flexibility of the American job market is extremely important in terms of enabling American businesses to continue to successfully compete in a worldwide economy.

But at the same time there is an increased desire for security and stability. A 2005 poll conducted by Nancy Wiefek found that when people were asked to choose between the opportunity to make money in the future and knowing their sources of income are protected, only 29 percent preferred opportunity and 62 percent selected stability.[33] There are very few "free agents" in today's labor force.

> There are very few "free agents" in today's labor force.

As recently as 2001, there was a sharp divide in how people defined job security. Some people thought of it the traditional way: a job with a large company or in civil service or as a tenured teacher where they would stay with that organization for a long, long time. But a different view evolved after the huge layoffs started in the 1980s; in this new view, a person's employer was seen as a personal "customer." Some concluded there was no security in having only one customer; they believed it was a safer life strategy to become your own "company" of one with five or six "customers."

A variation on that theme, popular in the business press for a while, was the idea of a free-floating labor force of educated entrepreneurs who would sell their services as opportunities appeared, and who would aggregate on projects and disaggregate when the project was finished. Few proponents of this view realized that a jobless labor force reflected the opportunities and optimism created by unusually good times and a stock market bubble in the second half of the 1990s.

It's hardly surprising that today the traditional view of security is far more widely held than the entrepreneurial one. Now most people want a job . . . and benefits . . . and a pension plan. College graduates of 2006 are demanding long-term benefits, including retirement plans and health insurance for dependents, even though most don't yet have dependents and are not old enough to even think of retiring! From a psychological viewpoint, it's a simple proposition: People who feel the world is basically chaotic and uncontrollable usually try to be part of an institution that is far stronger than they are as individuals.

SCARED, PASSIVE, AND CYNICAL

It is easy to see why many people feel alone, abandoned and ignored. Governments can't legislate job security without incurring major economic setbacks. There is little or no political or union leadership committed to the common good. No one seems willing to stand up to special interests. Elected politicians are scared of the media and worry more about publicity than about making good decisions and carrying them out.

There is no public discussion by any institutions about the issues that worry most people—loss of jobs, pensions, health insurance, and the quality of education. Why is this? Why isn't there an outcry about the eroding safety net? Increasingly, the public is passive—and cynical—about all of our institutions.

People are not worried about single issues like terrorism. They are frightened because they feel that they're all alone, trying to manage forces that are too big for them to control. While Americans are still basically self-reliant, they feel abandoned or ignored by their employer, their union, and their government.

People see their trust misplaced: governments did not rescue victims of Hurricane Katrina for days; the once-invincible GM and Ford laid off thousands of employees; and many companies are not meeting pension and healthcare obligations. This is particularly egregious when CEOs who were *fired* left their unsuccessful companies with extraordinary compensation packages.[34]

People are accustomed to hearing that the solution for rolling recessions, unstable industries, and organizational downsizing is "more education." So it is especially unsettling when they see people with advanced degrees and high-level skills in growth fields being laid off time after time. The reality message is that high levels of risk and instability are affecting even people who thought they were fully prepared, by education and experience, to succeed in a swiftly changing, more technical world. America's support for "creative destruction" is, very dramatically, good for the general economy, but it can fill individual lives with dread.

Mostly I worry because psychological insecurity has replaced psychological security for too many people. The American Dream, that uniquely American source of optimism, is in jeopardy.

CHAPTER TWELVE

A TWENTY-FIRST CENTURY
SAFETY NET

OVER THE PAST HALF-DOZEN YEARS, the American economic structure has faced horrendous setbacks: the financial fallout of the 9/11 attacks, the stock market crash, the dot-com implosion, and the recession. Yet our economy as a whole has demonstrated extraordinary resilience, productivity, and competitiveness. Looking at the overall picture, things are really pretty good. But they never were, and will never be, equally good for everyone.

One alarming outcome of heightened competition is that individuals and families may face unexpected perilous economic crises at any time.[1] This is the troubling reality. We have an obligation as a nation to protect people against calamity. It is, therefore, time for citizens and our political leaders to start the debate about safety nets. The central question is this: What would constitute necessary and healthy forms of protection? Be forewarned: there is no general agreement about any aspect of a safety net.

Every idea put forth about a new safety net is controversial to some vested interests who automatically push back against any change that threatens their own status quo. More fundamentally, there are huge philosophic differences between Democrats and Republicans or liberals and conservatives as to what they consider the proper role of government. Generally speaking, Democrats believe that expanding government supports a greater equity in outcomes, while Republicans believe that big government stifles self-reliance and the entrepreneurial spirit.

Only 65 percent of liberals are confident that sustained hard work and focus can enable people to overcome their disadvantages, in contrast to 92 percent of conservatives. This may explain the liberals' preoccupation with the wage gap between CEOs and average workers. Conservatives are less troubled by inequalities in the present because they are optimistic about people's chances to succeed in the future. The majority of CEOs, they point out, came from hard-working middle-class families. Even lower-income conservatives are twice as likely as upper-income liberals to believe the American Dream is relevant for everyone. In this sense, liberals could be viewed as generally pessimistic and conservatives basically optimistic about an individual's ability to move up the socio-economic ladder.[2]

> There are huge philosophic differences between Democrats and Republicans or liberals and conservatives as to what they consider the proper role of government.

Philosophical and perceptual differences this profound will inevitably lead to ideas that are fundamentally different in terms of how they work and the outcomes they are intended to bring about. That is why national discussions and ultimately debates about what should constitute a safety net in a globally interdependent economy are seriously necessary.

Harder times call for new ideas. Let the debates begin!

GOALS FOR A TWENTY-FIRST CENTURY SAFETY NET

Let me begin by laying out what a psychologist—rather than an economist or a politician—would like to see in or as an outcome of a twenty-first century safety net. Three things above all: it must reduce economic vulnerability and the paralyzing fear that goes along with it, it needs to bring back the optimism created by the hope-filled American Dream, and it must avoid a reinstatement of feelings of entitlement.

Goals

The first goal is to reduce the economic risks of individuals and families by creating policies and practices that prevent economic catastrophe in the face of health, death, or employment crises.

The second goal is to increase people's confidence, self-reliance, and resilience, and it is inextricably linked to the first. At the same time as it gives support against catastrophe, a safety net must also require that people achieve personal goals while receiving that support.

This requirement, which is the third goal, stems from the fact that when people don't have to earn what they get, they believe they are owed whatever they receive.[3] That attitude is called a Psychology of Entitlement and it results from too *much* protection from risk. Without risk and opportunities to learn how to handle it, people end up lacking confidence and are unable to cope with change. That's an awful personal quality at any time, and it's devastating in a world of accelerating change and risk.

Desirable characteristics of programs:

1. Vulnerable people's feelings of a Psychological Recession are diminished as major common risks are reduced.
2. To avoid feelings of entitlement, program benefits are earned by everyone in some way, such as through taxes (as in Social

Security or Medicare) or through effective and appropriate behavior (as in lower automobile insurance rates based on no accidents).

3. Program benefits involve individual choice and personal responsibility and reward positive behavior (i.e., a healthy lifestyle).

4. Programs foster personal initiative and self-reliance while they provide financial and other supports for economically vulnerable people and chronically low-income workers. (Example: Sustenance benefits like subsidized child care and/or housing can continue for a reasonable time for people actively in job training or low-wage entry jobs to give them time to move up and earn more.)

5. The costs and savings of benefit programs (medical bills, for example) are transparent and therefore understandable to beneficiaries.

6. Programs are simple for both users and administrators to understand and implement.

7. Programs make effective use of new technology tools to increase efficiency, cut costs, and decrease the size of the bureaucracy.

CRITICAL ELEMENTS OF A SAFETY NET

Given that thoughtful people can have many different ideas on what a safety net should comprise, I have my own vision of what are the most important elements: education, health care, and a new vision for management–employee collaboration. The discussion here, therefore, will focus on reforms in these three areas:

- a significantly improved K-12 education and an accessible, affordable program for adult learning
- healthcare changes that create widespread affordable coverage
- new relationships between employees and management that result in an increase in well-paying American jobs.

The discussion about a changed relationship between employees and management will be much shorter than the other two because this topic has been covered in Chapter 10, "Staying Ahead of the Curve." In addition, many creative voices offer a wide range of other risk-reducing programs including, for instance, new variations on insurance and changes in our tax structure. In this chapter, I simply present them briefly, as examples of things individuals, employers, and governments might choose to do.

EDUCATION REFORM

The United States cannot be successfully competitive in the international economy unless our labor force is smarter, more skilled, better educated, more innovative, and more productive than those of the competition. This goal can't be achieved without basic changes in the educational system, notably from kindergarten (or even preschool) through the 12th grade.

Like businesses, which are currently the most successful of our institutions, schools have to be customer-focused, results-driven meritocracies for students and teachers alike, in which only the most successful students earn recognition and the most successful teachers earn tenure and financial rewards.

The need for change in our public school system of K–12 education has become painfully self-evident. Our children do very poorly in international comparisons on tests of English and math, for example. The 20-point gap in performance levels between white and black students hasn't declined.[4] The money we spend on elementary and secondary education has increased by more than 50 percent since 1980, but reading scores for nine-year-olds have scarcely budged.[5]

Decades of pouring money into the *status quo* have not resulted in any significant academic gains in the K–12 public school system. The Department of Education's budget had increased six-fold from $14 billion in 1979, when it was created, to $90 billion in 2007, without any significant increase in our children's test performances.

Before they enter the public school system all children are eager learners; unfortunately in too many schools their experience makes them dislike learning as much as they're turned off by school itself.

A key part of a twenty-first century safety net is transmitting knowledge to children and giving them the ability to learn. Every child needs to become a person for whom learning and mastery are an essential source of pride and pleasure. The goals of learning and personal development should be the paramount goals of the first phase of education. Education in the twenty-first century has to create people who want to learn and who take life-long learning for granted. Anything less fails our children.

While it's really grand when children find learning to be fun, the educational system must also encourage and require high levels of self-discipline in regard to work, because too many children are not being required to perform or, worse, they are honored for simply showing up. There is a life lesson that has to be learned: children need to be taught that success is the outcome of hard work and that learning is, at this point in their life, their job.

> Children need to be taught that success is the outcome of hard work and that learning is, at this point in their life, their job.

I'm fascinated by my grandchildren's experience in a Montessori school. With 30 children, one teacher, and one assistant, and without any overt discipline, the classroom is silent except for a slight hum as every child is fully engrossed with whatever learning task, their work, they have chosen to perform this day.

At least as important as mastering the facts, children need to develop confidence in their abilities. This comes only from succeeding with challenging tasks. To the furthest extent possible, children's work needs to be individualized so that the level of achievement being required is a challenge but not an impossible one, so the child can have the joy of succeeding.

For the same reasons, schools need to end self-esteem programs in which children are rewarded simply to shore up their self-esteem, and they need to end social promotions. Children know how they are doing, and they know how all the other kids are doing. Every child who is doing poorly needs real help. Not addressing their real problems while shoving them under the proverbial rug through social promotion and unearned recognition assures their continued failure. That is not a favor.

The important personal qualities—confidence, resilience, and self-reliance—are not achieved without striving and then succeeding in something that is a manageable stretch. Every child is owed those opportunities.

Stupidity is doing the same old things and expecting a different result. With decades of futile efforts to improve outcomes in the educational establishment by simply increasing school budgets, it is more than time to create and experiment with fundamentally different approaches, especially those that have some track record of success.

All monopolies are inherently complacent, noncompetitive, and not oriented to their customer, and that includes the K–12 public school system. To break this cycle, America's public education needs what is known as disruptive change—changes in the basic rules of a system.

Just as in the business world, the cure for monopolistic lethargy in education is competition—for students, for money, for excellent faculty, for high test scores. Competition is what hones educational institutions toward excellence and genuine effective innovation.

To have some influence on school effectiveness, parents need the power of choice. Variations on school choice, such as vouchers and charter schools, are examples of disruptive changes. Both are important beginning innovations in breaking the educational monopoly. School vouchers allow students to attend private schools or charter schools, both of which, almost by definition, depart from the teaching style and curriculum of the public schools.

Charter schools are perhaps the most important innovation because they are built on people's passionate commitment to trying out their vision of academic excellence, while being held responsible for performance results. It is important to note that some charter schools have increased the school performance of minority children and enabled those kids to experience real success.[6]

Another break in the education establishment's monopoly-driven behavior will come when serious differentiations are made among teachers in terms of their effectiveness as measured by student performance. No one owns a job any more. Tenure—the right to hold a job for an entire career irrespective of poor performance—should never be as easily gained or as widely available as it is for K–12 teachers.

Some important and successful programs have effectively linked bonuses for teachers to improved performance by their underachieving students on standardized tests. The schools in Little Rock, Arkansas, offer us a strong example.

In 2005, teachers at Little Rock's Meadowcliff School, an inner-city grade school, were offered bonuses for improved student scores.[7] The dollar amount of the bonus increased in line with the size of the improvement: a four percent improvement in a child's test score resulted in a $100 bonus; a 15 percent improvement was rewarded with a $400 bonus. That first year, twelve teachers received bonuses ranging from $1,800 to $8,600.

The following year, Wakefield School joined Meadowcliff in the program. The bonus program there (and in the three other new participant schools) was based on the average improvement of a teacher's class rather than on a measurement of each child's performance. At the beginning of the academic year, Wakefield's students were in the 16th percentile, but they rose to the 29th percentile by the end of that year. In 2006, Wakefield's first year, its teachers earned $228,300 in bonuses; teachers at Meadow-cliff, then in its second year, earned $200,926. By 2007, five grammar schools were participating in the program.

Many experts believe that radical changes in the K–12 system are necessary in order to keep our population competitive in the world marketplace of jobs.[8] One prominent voice urging extreme changes comes from the New Commission on the Skills of the American Workforce, a bipartisan committee whose 26 members include New York Schools Chancellor Joel Klein, former cabinet secretaries, union representatives, and leaders from the corporate world.[9]

Recently, this commission issued a unanimous report that proposes a major shakeup in the way we educate children. The commission noted that despite a 240 percent increase in funding over the past 30 years, test scores of reading and math have barely moved from their low levels.

Among other ideas, the New Commission recommended:

- Ending high school for the majority of adolescents at age 16, after grade 10.

  Most kids who drop out do so because they are bored; this change would tend to prevent that. Students would not be permitted to leave school until they passed a state proficiency exam that complied with required national standards of achievement that demonstrate that students have world-class skills. After passing the exam most students would either go to a community college or into job training. Others could remain in high school and take advanced courses that prepared them to enter four-year colleges.
- Part of the money saved by eliminating the last two years of high school would be used to fund a year of preschool for all four-year-olds and all low-income three-year-olds.
- Another part of the newly available funds would be used to double teachers' salaries. The goal is to attract new graduates

who were in the top third of their college classes. Entry-level teachers would earn $45,000 a year, which could rise to $95,000 over the course of a career. In special circumstances teachers could earn up to $110,000.

In summary, America desperately needs

- An education that is relevant to today's children and teenagers.
- A K–12 system based on results.
- Merit increases for effective teachers and the freedom to fire ineffective ones.
- Increased school choices for K–12, including charter schools, vouchers, and tax credits for low-income students to attend private schools.

We would also greatly benefit from improvements in adult education. This would bring two benefits: working adults would have a way to bring their knowledge up to date, and parents would get help in creating a learning environment for their children.

Specific improvements in our adult educational system have been proposed:

- A new GI Bill available to veterans and other adults who meet relevant criteria.
- Flexible education accounts (i.e., a tax credit of up to $15,000 per decade) targeted especially to people in industries or specialties that have been affected by outsourcing or are simply in decline.
- Increased collaboration between employers and schools to customize programs, especially in community colleges, which are usually very effective and very affordable.
- Increased training and apprenticeship programs for all ages.
- More fellowships and scholarships based on merit.
- Assessments of current and future skill shortages and current and future growth industries to aid individuals and schools in planning.

In the best of all possible worlds, we could look forward to major curriculum changes from kindergarten through college, changes that would:

- Encourage innovation and creativity.
- Reinforce self-reliance as well as teamwork.
- Create knowledge about capitalism, investing, and handling money.
- Encourage life-long learning.
- Enhance civil behavior by focusing on civics and ethics.
- Nurture interpersonal as well as work-related skills.
- Increase leadership skills.

If all Americans were educated on that foundation, just imagine what we could achieve.

HEALTHCARE REFORM

No one doubts that America's healthcare system is a mess and needs major changes to ensure that everyone has access to affordable health care. As a result of decreased infant mortality and increased adult longevity, along with expensive improvements in medical technology and care, illness can easily become a financial catastrophe.

For decades, we have thought of healthcare funding as something provided (more or less) by employers. It has been taken for granted for so long that many do not realize this employer-based system got started for a purely practical reason. Because of wage controls in effect during World War II, employers of that era couldn't reward people with greater pay. So they substituted increased benefits, because these were not limited by government fiat and, as a major added bonus, were not taxed as income. That worked reasonably well during a period when people tended to spend their entire working life with one employer. We all know that is increasingly no longer true.

The number of people who are insured through their employer is declining, as the premiums keep rising and fewer employers are offering health insurance. The percentage of employees who are covered by employer plans fell from 81.2 percent in 2001 to 77.4 percent in 2005.[10] Even among companies that still offer health care, many are offering reduced coverage while shifting some of the costs to employees.

While the tendency among younger people, especially, is to move from employer to employer as opportunities arise and circumstances dictate, about 175 million Americans continue to get their health insurance through their employer. Only about 27 million purchase it directly, on their own.[11] For a variety of reasons, not all of which have to do with poverty, 46 million Americans have no health insurance.

Even those who do have coverage at work are not free of anxiety. Many are worried they could lose health benefits if they change jobs. People are afraid that if premiums continue to rise, the company will simply end their coverage. Many fear for their very jobs, as employers use layoffs to counterbalance soaring benefits costs.

From the corporation's point of view, they have little choice but to cut back. Health benefits make up almost half (44 percent) of all spending on benefits; in actual dollars, health benefits have doubled in just five years, from $94.2 billion in 2000 to $183.3 billion in 2005.[12] A big part of the problem is that our healthcare delivery system is woefully inefficient, costing 16 percent of our gross domestic product compared with 10.6 percent in Germany and eight percent in Japan.[13]

> Several very powerful constituencies are calling for major changes in the American healthcare system, which suggests that some change is likely to occur within the next few years.

More and more, business is complaining that the cost of providing health insurance for their employees and the extra cost levied on them to cover the "free" care that hospitals are required to give are making them noncompetitive with companies from countries where business is not the source of health insurance. Several very powerful constituencies are, therefore, calling for major changes in the American healthcare system, which suggests that some change is likely to occur within the next few years.

Few people argue with the fundamental changes that are needed to our current healthcare system. Healthcare costs need to come down; health insurance has to be portable, tied to the person and not the place of employment; and health insurance needs to cover people with preexisting conditions, as well as people with low incomes.

But the strategies suggested to accomplish these goals differ widely, separated largely by the philosophic foundations of liberals and conservatives and their very different views of large government as the means to effectively solve problems.

Shoring Up the Employer-Based System

There are currently three basic approaches to solving America's healthcare problems: one approach favors bigger government; a second view is to build on the existing employer-based system; and the third view is to rely less on government and more on market forces in which people would buy their own health insurance and receive financial help if that were necessary.

Big government, a single-payer national system such as exists in Canada and Britain, is viewed with enthusiasm by a minority of Democrats. Senator Ted Kennedy would like to expand Medicare to children and adults aged 55 to 64 as a step to covering all Americans. That doesn't seem likely, given that Canada and Britain's national systems are experiencing rising costs and long waits with wealthier people turning to the private sector for their health care.

Most Democrats want to retain the existing employer-based system and use expanded government programs as a relatively simple and inexpensive way to gain health coverage for the uninsured.

Two Republicans, former Massachusetts governor Mitt Romney and California's Governor Arnold Schwarzenegger, have suggested plans designed to build on the existing health insurance offered by employers. The Massachusetts plan is now a law; California's is in play with the state legislature.

In both plans, all residents would be required to have health insurance. Employers who don't offer health insurance would pay an assessment to the state.[14] Those assessments would be used to provide for the uninsured, who could get health insurance through offerings from the state or a subsidy to help purchase it. In addition to assessments on businesses, California's plan includes new taxes on doctors and hospitals to help pay for the state's 6.5 million uninsured people.

Some states, like Maine and Vermont, have already enacted universal coverage plans. Currently, 15 other states, including Wisconsin, Minnesota, Illinois, Kansas, and Pennsylvania, are considering them. Financing often builds on mandatory employer-offered insurance, requirements that the uninsured buy insurance, subsidies for low-income people, and government-subsidized insurance pools to lower costs and share risks.

Less Government and More Free Market Forces

In President George W. Bush's 2007 State of the Union Address he took a new approach to managing health care. He proposed using tax deductions to get more people to buy health insurance and looked to competition among health insurance providers to get the cost of insurance down.

At present, the majority of Americans get their health insurance from their employers, which leads to great differences in coverage among people with different employers. It also leads people to be ignorant of and uninvolved with the actual costs of their medical treatments. In the present system, there's no reason for people who receive employer-based insurance to curtail their medical spending since it feels free to them.[15] At the same time, businesses can deduct the cost of employee health insurance but individuals cannot. This means that people who purchase their own insurance have no advantage except portability.

The plan the Republicans are proposing would give individuals a standard deduction of $7,500 (and families, $15,000) for health insurance regardless of whether it was paid for by the individual or the individual's employer. As the average employer-based family health insurance plan costs about $11,500 a year and the tax deduction would be $15,000 irrespective of what the insurance actually cost, most families would come out ahead, with the families who buy their own insurance benefiting the most.

This new tax break is intended to help low-income families buy health insurance. At the same time, with the objective of getting medical costs lower, people whose health plans are more expensive than the national average would be liable for additional taxes.

Under the Republican plan, the majority of low-wage and middle-income people would have lower health insurance costs. The present system favors the well-to-do, families earning over $100,000 that receive an average tax subsidy of $2,780. Families whose members earned $30,000 or less received less than $725 in subsidized help.[16]

The Republican plan is based on a consumer-driven system and the outcomes of a competitive market. From this point of view, it would be very desirable for state-limited markets to open up to a national health insurance market. Individuals who now buy their own health insurance can only buy in a single-state market. One result is that insurers have little incentive to develop innovative new products.

If the new tax treatment encourages more people to buy their own portable health insurance, several positive outcomes are likely: people will develop greater awareness of the actual costs, an enlarged market for private purchasers could encourage price competition among insurers, and companies will have reason to develop new kinds of plans.

New Ideas and Different Views

At long last, the United States may be ready to tackle a real over-haul of its healthcare system. In itself, that will generate a wide range of ideas, some of which will be both innovative and effective.

One such proposal has been put forth by Ezekiel Emanuel, chairman of the Department of Clinical Bioethics at the National Institutes of Health, and Victor Fuchs, a professor of economics at Stanford University.[17] They propose a plan that will support Americans' preference for individually based choices in a universal healthcare plan. This approach will also ease the financial burden on business. They call for:

- A universal voucher for people who are younger than 65 that pays for a core benefit package like those currently offered by employers.
- Choice of a health plan and physicians. People who want greater coverage, especially by specialists, would be free to purchase those options.
- The funding would be taken care of by an earmarked value added tax (VAT) of about 10 percent. This is not additional money; these funds replace employer tax breaks and the funds spent on employer-based care and Medicaid.
- Creation of a Health Care Fed, akin to the Federal Reserve System, to evaluate the care people are receiving and the benefits of new technology.
- Malpractice reform through a new Center for Patient Safety and Dispute Resolution that would evaluate patient claims of medical incompetence, compensate patients if appropriate, and disqualify incompetent practitioners.

Emanuel and Fuchs believe their voucher system would eliminate the connection between being employed and being medically covered. This system also relieves business of the $650 billion a year that it spends on health care, relieves the states of administering Medicaid and other means-tested systems, and allows for Medicare and its taxes to be phased out. Because people dislike paying taxes, there is some limit to the size of the VAT and greater health care services. A universal healthcare voucher, they believe, would solve most of the problems created by the present system.

As I write this (early 2007), it is anybody's guess what will become of these various proposals. But one thing is clear: *something has to change.*

A NEW VISION FOR COLLABORATION

For too long, too many organizations have rested uneasily on a foundation that is cracking under the sustained tension between management and employees. We've all seen it: lunchrooms full of people complaining bitterly about the boss, open disdain from managers about their team members, and employees blogging their resent about the company. It seems almost an automatic response: Employees see the manager as evil, management sees the employees as lazy. This sense of enmity is most obvious in some unionized workplaces, but it is by no means limited to them. Too often, across all industries, there is a pervasive sense in both groups that each is the other's main enemy.

> The enemy is external —companies that are poised to take business away from us. What we need now is to replace that automatic conflict with a new spirit of collaboration.

That must change. We cannot afford internal adversarial relationships among people in the same organization. Honest disagreements that lead to better solutions are constructive; internal squabbling is destructive. Everyone, top to bottom, needs to face up to this reality: the enemy is external—companies that are poised to take business away from us. Every company needs to pull together to head off this threat. What we need now is to replace that automatic conflict with a new spirit of collaboration.

Aerospace giant Boeing has discovered that giving up one-way control is a good thing. It has begun using blogs to create *open dialogues* with employees, the public, and its customers. The goal is to explain the company and begin to really communicate internally as well as externally.[18]

The first Boeing blog was started in 2005 by Randy Baseler, a vice-president for marketing who wanted to communicate Boeing's view of the commercial airplane industry. He was swiftly criticized by his blog readers for not allowing them to comment on what he was saying. Instead of fleeing from negative feedback, Baseler hung in and he learned. His analysis of the differences in strategy between Airbus and Boeing was particularly enlightening, and his Web log attracted 30,000 visitors in April 2006.

Criticism almost always exists. The question is, do you want to know what it says? Boeing has learned that the benefit of knowing and addressing criticism far outweighs ignoring or silencing it. The company is now creating blog kiosks to gain input about new strategies or policies from its leaders even during important meetings where they're being discussed. And Boeing's executives are becoming convinced that encouraging employee openness is the way to go. They have created ways for employees to communicate anonymously on company blogs. Only when all the issues are out on the table can dialogue and problem solving begin.

In a very competitive world, bickering and in-fighting are simply too expensive. A great deal of time and resources are bound up in these nonproductive activities. Even worse, organizations characterized by internal warfare are rarely productive, much less innovative. Today, any company that can't beat the competition finds itself quickly out of business. And beating the competition requires everyone pulling in the same direction, not being at cross purposes. As difficult as it might be to achieve, today's organizations need partnerships between management and employees who respect, trust, and value the others while they focus on achieving the goals and surpassing the prior performance of the company.

Collaboration is much easier to achieve when every participant is keenly aware that cooperating could result in something really good while continued conflict could have a disastrous outcome. In 1997 Toyota faced a terrifying production crisis— the factory that was the primary producer of a critical part, a brake valve, was destroyed by fire. The situation was potentially catastrophic because Toyota excelled in lean, just-in-time manufacturing and most of its factories had only a four-hour supply of the valve in-house.[19] Building a new factory would take half a year, during which time Toyota's production of 14,000 cars a day would simply stop.

With Toyota and every member of its network having something really serious at risk, the company reached out to its suppliers to come up with a solution. About 200 companies in Toyota's network collaborated with one another, and they came up with six different production solutions that used very different approaches, tools, and organizational structures. Engineers and managers who were normally competitors worked together across the network. In the amazing time of five days, production of the critical valves was fully ongoing; in one week, production was equal to the levels before the fire. With collaboration, production was saved and so were jobs and companies.

Union shops, of course, represent in some people's minds the biggest challenge for a collaborative workplace. Here is the enlightening example of the city of Indianapolis.

In 1992, Stephen Goldsmith was elected mayor of Indianapolis, Indiana. Mayor Goldsmith wanted to privatize the delivery of city services and its operations. At that time, almost half of the city's workers were in public-sector unions, specifically the American Federation of State, County, and Municipal Employees (AFSCME). In the face of the new mayor's privatization threat, the city's workers went scrambling for a better alternative. The end result was a successful reform of the city's departments, bringing a new, collaborative partnership between employees and management that improved performance and lowered costs.[20]

The Indianapolis model of partnership encourages both cooperation and competition between the city's departments and private contractors. In this case, creating collaboration required the continuation of collective bargaining to increase employee's trust and buy-in. Traditional collective bargaining continues on issues like hours and wages, and collaboration is the hallmark of efforts to improve quality, costs, customer relationships, and the development of neighborhoods.

In other words, employees and managers were able to direct efforts toward their separate concerns while also jointly pursuing their common goals and competing successfully against private suppliers. This successful collaboration between employees and management has been able to meet the needs of the city's organizations and the people who work in them and has resulted in enduring partnerships between the constituencies.

While replacing adversarial relationships with collaborative ones can be difficult and take considerable time, the payoff is worth it. Consider next the tale of two cities, Detroit and Pittsburgh.

In 1951, a little more than a half century ago, the United States had two-thirds of the world's manufacturing capacity and produced 60 percent of the world's oil and 66 percent of its steel.[21] Americans were five percent of the world's population, but they were wealthier than the other 95 percent combined. And Americans produced almost everything that Americans consumed, including their cars. In 1954, 99.93 percent of all cars sold in this country were American brands, built mostly in Detroit, the Motor City.

> When you have been at the top of the heap for decades, it is almost impossible to believe you're not there any more.

The changes in the industry started in the 1970s when foreign cars, notably those from Japan and Germany, began to gain market share in the United States because of startlingly better quality. By the end of the decade, the Big Three automakers were already in serious trouble, although none would admit it.

Denial is not just a river in Egypt.

When you have been at the top of the heap for decades, it is almost impossible to believe you're not there any more, despite a reality that tells you were but now you're not.

America's automakers and the UAW are a classic example of denial, of continued complacency despite shrinking market share and flowing red ink. For years, management and the union shared the vice of motivated denial in the face of a radically changed, vastly more internationally competitive industry.

The psychology of entitlement, or a deep-seated complacency, was particularly ingrained in the automobile industry. Because denial feels much more comfortable and safer than stepping up to basic change, complacency is immensely difficult to change, and that was particularly true in insular Detroit.

By 1980, during a fierce recession and increasing prices for energy and labor, at least some people at Ford and the UAW realized that major changes were necessary and achieving them would require collaboration between the union and management.[22]

This collaboration was realized in the development of a world-class lean manufacturing system set up to produce the Duratec engine in Cleveland Engine Plant No. Two. Hundreds of union members worked with Ford management and engineers for more than two years using self-managed teams to create just-in-time production and the most thorough employee development and training systems in the industry. This enormous investment was highly successful and should have become the template for the future, for Ford and the rest of the industry.

Instead, American automobile executives continued to ignore the importance of manufacturing quality and the UAW leadership elected to oppose innovations that increased quality and productivity. Complacency is a terrible liability in the face of radical change: its outcomes are measured in oceans of red ink.

Now to Pittsburgh. Around 1983 I worked as a consultant for Westinghouse's Nuclear Fuels Division and that work brought me to Pittsburgh. The city had been a center of steel manufacturing for years, but that industry was in serious decline.

When I arrived, I found it hard to believe the miles of empty, closed steel mills. The old steel industry was dying, and so was the city.

Today, Pittsburgh boasts modern, efficient, specialized mini-mills. The improvement in productivity is noteworthy. By 2005 the steel industry was producing more product than in the 1980s even though the number of workers was down by two-thirds. Constructive job cutting saved the entire industry.[23]

Both industries and both cities were victims of high labor costs. After 25 years of an increasingly competitive economy, it is inescapable that no company, no industry, and no nation can afford disproportionately high costs, including the price of labor.

Union membership is in decline in many nations. In the 1950s, about 35 percent of American workers were union members. Since then that membership has been declining, and in 2006 it slid down to 12 percent. Sticking to their traditional adversarial position with management has led unions, generally speaking, to cut off their noses to spite their faces. With the exception of the teachers' and civil service unions, unions have become irrelevant to the majority of American workers.

In the heyday of American unions during the 1950s and 1960s, union power enabled ordinary workers to rise to middle-class prosperity. In those decades, the majority of workers hadn't finished high school and most worked in repetitive jobs where they were expected to leave their brains at the door. Today, two-thirds of workers are high school graduates and many have some college education. They are expected to think and innovate in collaboration with management in order for their business to succeed.

Smart employees do not find the traditional union anti-boss message relevant. Unions became weak and unable to protect their members when they resisted acknowledging and adapting to fundamental changes in a global economy as well as profound changes in the education demographics of Americans.

The largest, most effective, and most productive safety net is a healthy, expansive, job- and wealth-creating economy. Anything that interferes with that outcome is counterproductive. To become relevant and effective in a competitive economy, unions need to accept the need to be flexible and innovative; rigid labor rules and bloated compensation make their organizations noncompetitive.

Even in manufacturing, it can be done. In 2006, U.S. factory production of audio and video equipment increased by 23 percent; even production of major appliances increased.[24] Manufacturers who produce really high-end products that are customized locally and who have specialized niche markets will often find it can be better to be near the customer than outsource production. That's especially the case when labor is contributing its knowledge to improve quality and productivity.

> To become relevant and effective in a competitive economy, unions need to accept the need to be flexible and innovative.

The unions' goal, like that of owners, management, and employees, is to create stronger businesses that beat the competition, keep most jobs at home, and ultimately hire more people. It is in the unions' best interest to improve customer outcomes, productivity, and profits. Union leaders and members need to collaborate with management just as management must collaborate with unions in achieving an organization's—or an industry's—success.

Costco is an example of a management that supports its employees generously and works with Costco's Teamsters Negotiations Committee to keep employees at the top of the retail industry in terms of wages and benefits.[25] In early 2007, Costco's full-time workers averaged $17 an hour and the company paid more than 92 percent of the employees' health insurance. Oh, yes, Costco is significantly more profitable and its workers are significantly more productive than those at Wal-Mart, as detailed in Chapter 5.

MORE IDEAS ABOUT
A MODERN SAFETY NET

The nation needs a modern safety net, especially for the many people who will, at times, find themselves adrift, losers in the turmoil of a rapidly changing economy. We need to continue those policies that have led to broad economic gains, but we also need to provide aid for those who were left behind and those who are newly vulnerable. Because major changes in the economy can now affect anyone, the new safety net must include everyone, from the factory floor to well-educated knowledge workers.

Some ideas that have been proposed include:

- Wage insurance for displaced employees that would make up part of the difference in earnings in a new job for two years.*[26]
- Catastrophe insurance in case of death of a spouse, disability, a major drop in income, or a medical crisis.*
- A federally mandated higher minimum wage.[27]
- A higher earned income tax credit.
- Pension insurance.
- Tax incentives for businesses to stay in the United States and for workers to retrain.*
- A 401(k) plan for low- and middle-income earners in which the government would match the first $2,000 of savings up to two-to-one.*
- All newborns from the middle- and lower-income classes would receive from $500 to $1,000 in investment accounts that could accept other contributions—contributions to poor children's accounts would be matched by government—and would grow tax-free.*
- Health savings plans and other new forms of health insurance.[28]

Many of these ideas are designed to reduce the risk of individuals by creating interventions in which some of the risk is shared by large numbers of people through taxes. An important indirect outcome of such programs would be the reinstatement of people's sense of being part of a large and caring community. I am certain this would help greatly in replacing fear with hope.

The current level of fear is far too great and has led to a deep pessimism and a scary passivity, the result of expecting the worst and feeling helpless to do anything about it. In the short term, we need to provide more help to people whose jobs are lost to a more global economy. And, instead of fear, we need a focused sense of urgency. To achieve these things, we need leaders who are able to communicate the fact that while individuals may experience more risk than they used to, a rising tide lifts all boats and as the economic pie is growing larger so are opportunities for the majority of people. The reasons for optimism far outweigh those for pessimism.

CHAPTER THIRTEEN

PSYCHOLOGY IS MORE IMPORTANT THAN ECONOMICS

A T THIS POINT IN OUR HISTORY, fear is eclipsing reality. In a vague, collective way, as a nation we seem to have concluded that Chicken Little is right, the sky *is* falling and *the end is near!*

The problem is, that's not true. While we can't take success for granted and we must sustain an entrepreneurial business climate, we remain the most entrepreneurial and innovative economy to date. These widespread apocalyptic expectations need a major course correction. To get there, we need a better understanding of human psychology much more than we need improvement in the numbers.

The fear driving so much of our lives today is deep and visceral, but it is not new. The 1870s was a parallel era in our history and it shines a light on the deep sources of our current fearful state.[1]

In July 1877, angry mobs of railroad workers created an inferno in the Pennsylvania Railroad yard, trapping a unit of state militiamen who fought their way out with a Gatling gun. Over the next several weeks, riots raged all over the country from New York to San Francisco. Historians have explained this social turmoil as the result of a great depression during the decade. But more recent analyses revealed that, except for a brief recession in 1873, the era was not a period of economic decline, but instead perhaps the fastest period of sustained growth of jobs and consumption in our history.

Why, then, would people be so upset and agitated? Like now, the 1870s was also a time of a new and borderless economy, and many people had good reason to be scared. The railroads and the telegraph had spread and the mail brought catalogues from huge department store chains, forcing many local stores out of business. In the midwest, huge factory farms worked by teams of 70 horses pulling enormous plows overwhelmed smaller farm operations. Even these large farms, which often dominated world markets, were not immune to trouble. Grain markets were global and volatile, and great crops on the Russian steppes could wipe out American farmers' profit for that year.

In addition, the unfettered entrepreneurialism of the period gave rise to robber barons and a great gap between the fantastically rich and everyone else.

Both geographic and social mobility soared. While the nation as a whole enjoyed a large increase in the overall standard of living, for many people the anchor to windward, the feeling of being moored to a family, to a place, to an employer or an enterprise, was gone. The sense of stability, of belonging, of knowing what you could count on, of fairness and equity, all were jeopardized during this period of economic boom and fundamental change.

Many pundits are pondering the mystery of why, in the middle of an economy that has been strong for five years, so many view their world through a half-empty lens. There is no mystery; the answer lies less with economics than with psychology.

The American meritocracy, the principle of being valued for what you have personally achieved, grants us the freedom to become whatever we can be. But that freedom can also generate a critical amount of insecurity when many significant factors are simultaneously in flux.

Competition keeps increasing between companies in different countries and between companies within a country. The result is a sense of huge, amorphous threats. For Americans, they include China, India, Singapore, Malaysia, Eastern Europe, downsizing, rightsizing, outsourcing, layoffs, flat wages, and health insurance and pension benefits gone or in jeopardy. The reality is inescapable: people in different industries with different specialties are vulnerable to economic trauma even if they are well educated, skilled, knowledgeable, and experienced.

The list of woes is woefully familiar; familiar because these threats to the optimism-creating American Dream are repeated endlessly without any recognition that good things are also going on.

The great majority of American jobs are still not likely to be shipped overseas because the costs and difficulties involved in managing an overseas operation are high and American workers are at least as skilled as and often more productive than other groups.[2] It is true that the Fortune 500 lost five million jobs from 1980 through 2000, *but* 34 million new jobs were added to the economy from entrepreneurial smaller companies. The strongest source of jobs in the United States has always come from newer and less visible companies.

The facts are largely positive, but at the moment the facts don't seem to matter very much. What does matter is what we perceive and anticipate because that forms what we unconsciously select to see and hear and believe. There is no balance in the messages we receive in all of the media about job losses, growing international strength, and our national vulnerability. Economists have been saying wage and benefit increases will follow—and they have—after a surge in the number of jobs. But few people have heard that because the pessimistic view dominates.

Overwhelmingly, the facts support the view that in the global competition we remain tremendously strong and vital. Yes, China has a huge trade balance and India supports lots of call centers, *but the world economies are growing larger.* This is not a zero-sum game in which we lose as some jobs migrate. No one in the media is discussing this, and very few people know or understand it.

> Overwhelmingly, the facts support the view that in the global competition we remain tremendously strong and vital.

Our current national sense of vulnerability is heightened because of what preceded it. The post-World War II period of American hegemony was largely the result of the destruction of Japan as well as much of Europe. That world no longer exists. As the global economy grows, our share will diminish. While we are very likely to lead in productivity in certain industries, we will no longer be the leader in all of them. Competition for customers will continue to increase for every entrant in all economies. Everyone will have to work much smarter—and we can.

The U.S. economy emerged as strong and resilient after the crises of 2000 to 2002. With a tight labor market, a very low unemployment rate, and no significant inflation, it is surprising that the result hasn't been widespread confidence and good feelings about the future. But the nation is uneasy. There is a familiar dolorous list of woes: Iraq, terrorism, rising costs for fuel, health care, college, and wage stagnation.

It's easy to understand why too many people are carrying black umbrellas though the sun is shining. It's scary when it feels like the rock you've always stood on has been replaced by shifting sands. Although people are certainly upset by specific issues, like the war in Iraq or high gasoline prices, *the real core of what they're worried about is the quality of their future.* A fatalistic view of what's coming and an inability to control it are much scarier than acknowledging the price of gasoline and deciding to drive less. And Americans are also personalizing what's happening, pointing to inept leadership, but the loss of job security and increased competition are happening everywhere to everyone.

The basic debate seems to be on the question of whether the sky has already fallen or, if not, when will it fall. No one seems to be asking how far up it will go. Exaggerated gloom pervades despite reality, and this negative view is deep and entrenched. It has permeated both political parties and sometimes the Fed and the White House.[3] With almost no signs that anyone in a leadership position really cares about the welfare of people, it is no wonder that there's widespread anxiety.

Our doom and gloom viewpoint is dangerous because it leads to more caution than boldness at a time when it's imperative to wrestle with hard issues and make major changes. It is vital to have perspective. We have lived through some horrific challenges— 9/11, rate hikes, high energy prices, and Hurricane Katrina—and yet our economy remains vibrant. The nation needs to revive its conviction that Americans do cope, labor is flexible and innovative, and the basic economy is strong.

> Our doom and gloom viewpoint is dangerous.

AMERICA'S STRENGTHS

At a time when the world is a hard and judgmental task master, the basis of competitive advantage lies in people who are resilient and creative and a society that is innovative and transparent. These are America's strengths. They are the legacy of our history, and they are hard to replicate or graft onto other cultures.

Americans hold certain values with an almost spiritual faith as guidelines for behavior, and to "become Americanized" is to embrace these views. We believe in the rule of law and equal opportunity, of freedom of speech, thought, and religion, and most of all, we believe in individual liberty. We may share these values with other people, but our belief in them is especially strong. Taken as a whole, these beliefs and attributes will contribute to our future success and competitiveness.

America's advantage lies in certain basic beliefs, beginning with the notion that you achieve your status and *failure is not a permanent state*. In the crucible of a meritocracy in which status is earned rather than inherited, there is no permanent shame in having tried and failed. The only lasting shame is in not having tried; from a very young age Americans learn, *Try, try, and try again*.

Confidence largely develops from opportunities to meet and conquer challenges, problems that are new to us. We learn more from stumbling and recovering than from honing well-practiced skills. The fact that any stumble can be regarded as a bump in a positive road allows large numbers of Americans to develop self-confidence, and it is self-confidence that underlies the quality of resilience, the ability to pull yourself together and reenter the arena. In a demanding, swiftly changing competitive world, resilience will be ever-increasingly important.

Confidence and resilience are largely the result of our personal freedoms, including the freedom to make decisions and pursue whatever options we choose. People are, therefore, held responsible for their choices and the quality of their judgments. That, in combination with the view that *there is no free lunch*, means you're responsible for yourself.

We believe in a meritocracy, an open society in which upward mobility is the reward for work. America has more income mobility than any other country, which is why we've never had class warfare.[4] Almost 86 percent of people in the lowest quintile of income in 1979 were no longer in the bottom group by 1988. On the other extreme, almost 53 percent of the people who were in the top one percent of income in 1979 were no longer in that group a decade later. Income mobility means that people with little income can realistically aspire to become part of the upper groups, and they often succeed. The Psychological Recession reflects anxiety and fear about what might happen in the future; it does not reflect conflict between haves and have-nots.

America is a place that was settled by people who came from somewhere else, who kept going west for the sheer possibilities that were offered, for whom the open road—the freedom to move away from or move toward—is a metaphor for personal freedom. People's potential, in this view, cannot be limited by their status or that of their family. So we work harder and longer than most other nations in part because we're striving upward and in part because we also see work as a virtue in itself.

We believe in the value of individualism, and we also believe in respect for individuals. They are not the same thing. A focus on individualism diminishes the emphasis on groups, thus on conformity and group-speak. Most major advances come from the work of individuals. We Americans like mavericks, people whose views diverge from that of the majority. This value lets people feel comfortable while being different. Since we expect different opinions from different people, we prefer those opinions be on the table because we see constructive disagreement as a way to achieve transparency, trust, and innovation.

Respect for individuals is a value that says all people of all socioeconomic classes and colors and ethnicities and national origins and physical characteristics have the right to earn respect and be included. Many groups in the United States have had to fight for acceptance but, over time, they do. And many of us are only a generation or two removed from our immigrant forebears who came from everywhere and brought their fierce opinions with them. We know that courageous, motivated, opinionated immigrants from all over the world have always been a major source of energy to this country.

In the global economy, being able to collaborate with many different kinds of people and being mentally free to see the world differently will be critical for success. The combination of the dual values of individualism and respect for individuals allows Americans to be both singular individuals and team players. Individualism is the basis for creative breakthroughs and teamwork makes seamless, effective innovation possible.

When individualism and respect for individuals are combined with the freedom and responsibility to speak out and air differences, the opportunities for trust increase greatly. Developing trust becomes a critical variable when people deal with others whose backgrounds, perspectives, and values are very different. Without trust, there is no possibility of joint collaboration.

Americans don't revere history. Unlike many nations we tend not to preserve what's old just because it's old. We're not tradition bound. Our unique identity as Americans is based on individualism and not on a historical collective mindset. The Declaration of Independence grants us all the right to "life, liberty, and the pursuit of happiness." Our founding fathers gave us individual rights including the pursuit of happiness and that, says *The Economist*, is what makes us different.[5]

In the United States, you don't often hear "we've always done it this way" as a rationalization against change. We value what's more effective or productive. In other words, we have a penchant to look forward and not backward, which makes it easier for us than many others to embrace creative destruction and risky entrepreneurialism.

Because we don't idealize the past and look to it as a source of solutions to tomorrow's problems, we tend to be open to what's new, adaptive, and flexible. We are also prone to pragmatism, much more concerned with making things work than with the philosophy of how things should be.

THE THREAT FROM OTHER COUNTRIES

The opposite of the bad coin of complacency is panic, sustained high levels of fear. The eminent columnist Robert Samuelson has noted that Americans are prone to panic about every 15 to 20 years.[6] Many watched the launch of Sputnik in 1957 and said it meant America would be dominated by the Soviet Union. In the late 1970s and the 1980s, we were certain to lose our competitive position, first to Germany and then to Japan. Now we're told that China and India, which are graduating many thousands more engineers and scientists than we are, will gobble all of the manufacturing jobs and anything else that can be moved beyond our national borders.

China, India, Russia, and their ilk are the new bogeymen, but they will not outpace us swiftly or easily. The reason is the very heart of their existence as conformist or totalitarian nations. Divergent thinking is key to creativity. Today's conditions dictate that the winning competitor is one that can create new products or systems or customers. Totalitarian and conformist states, in contrast, reject outsiders and divergent opinions and enforce group-think of the masses.

As the grandchild of four immigrants, I am always thrilled by the diversity of Americans. The outsiders, our immigrants, hungry and motivated to create better lives for themselves and their children, have always been a major part of the engine of our economic growth. The engine of innovation is one of the things we do best, and it is fueled by a surge of new ideas from all directions, including those who came here from afar.

We are a wealthy developed country but we also manage to have some of the characteristics of a scrappy, open, flexible, gutsy developing nation that doesn't care much about tradition and history.[7] This energy and ambition, our willingness to work harder than people in other rich countries, has, as one of its origins, our continuous renewal and rebirth created by the millions of immigrants from different cultures, all united by their fierce desire to succeed.

> We are a wealthy developed country but we also manage to have some of the characteristics of a scrappy, open, flexible, gutsy developing nation.

In 1999, for example, immigrants created about one-fourth of the new tech companies in Silicon Valley.[8] In 2005, that percentage had increased to 52 percent. In that year, immigrants who became entrepreneurs, most notably people from India, employed 450,000 people and generated $52 billion in sales. The immigrants' contribution to American innovativeness as well as to the economy is immense.

The great majority of students in the Indian subcontinent, the Far East, Latin American, and Eastern Europe are very, very good at memorizing. But they are not good at challenging peers or authority, or perceiving and thinking differently, or diverging from what is currently widely accepted and conveyed by their governments.

These students are very good at implementing what is already known and improving what is already approved. But they are very limited in their ability to see differently and create basic new solutions and opportunity out of problems.

Both India and China have become aware that while they are becoming operationally very good, they are not fostering innovation in their educational systems. In their view that is the result of too much technical training—math and science—and too little in the arts and humanities. They also realize that one root of their dearth of creativity is the policy of not challenging authority, including teachers.[9]

America's colleges and universities are free from government intervention and censorship and they compete vigorously among themselves for the best students, professors, and ideas. They are energized and ambitious and it shows: Of the top 10 universities in the world, eight are American.[10] Of the top 20 universities in the world 18 are in the U.S.[11]

In our good public and private schools, colleges, and universities, students are challenged to learn and then view things differently. Students are taught to identify and question assumptions and challenge conclusions. They're praised when they present alternatives, albeit politely, to their teachers. We reward individualism and see memorization and group-think as the death of thinking.

Innovation is not encouraged in totalitarian or corrupt states because nonconformist thought is seen as a threat to those in power. Corruption makes transparency impossible, increasing people's fear of being out of line. In nondemocratic political systems, political, military, and economic power are held by a single group, and differences of thought or action are prohibited and severely punished. In contrast, democracies foster different views by having more than one political party, and different political groups always disagree with each other.

Totalitarian states are never transparent. They fear the actions of dissidents because they spread destabilizing ideas. And in nondemocratic states, like China and Russia, the system is never transparent because of a long history of widespread corruption and nominally illegal practices by which the powerful control and rape the powerless.

While Russia and China have enjoyed tremendous economic success in the past decade or two, the extent of their future success may be blunted by crippling cultural conditions: widespread corruption, especially at the local level; lack of personal freedom; government-controlled media; and the absence of free, open, and transparent markets.

Certain conditions are essential to a free marketplace: buyers, sellers, and investors need a free flow of information. That requires freedom of speech, freedom to write and publish, and, most especially, freedom to think the truth as you see it without punishment.[12] Personal freedom leading to individual creativity, and trust created through the transparency of the entire system, are critical to success in the borderless world.

In all of the rhetoric describing the great threats to America's future, there is virtually no mention of the need for individual rights to develop personal and social resilience; or the need for intellectual and political freedom to achieve creativity and innovation; or the need for transparency to create trust among diverse people in the midst of rapid change. Along all those dimensions, America shines. It is therefore, not surprising that the United States is a leader in creating innovation and in commercializing it.[13]

In other words, totalitarian states cannot be among the most economically successful societies because in those cultures there are no individual rights or individualism. Only democratic societies have a free press and encourage or tolerate dissension.

Our universities and research centers embrace both intellectual freedom and integrity to the extent that the entire community takes those values for granted. The only milieu in which experimental, cutting-edge breakthroughs can happen is that in which the major commitment is to the pursuit of truth and those who seek it are genuinely free to explore. These institutions, together with a noncorrupt government, regulated and transparent financial markets, and the rule of law, have made us strong.

LOSE THE FEAR AND RELEASE THE ENERGY!

What about the future? In the political sphere, we have a failure of leadership. When politicians are self-indulgent in their partisanship, as ours currently are, they create purposeless divisiveness.

In the face of enormous political issues, there is no national will. Where is the sense of mission, of urgency about solving major issues—immigration, health care, education, energy, and deficits? Given that the size of the total labor force has doubled to three billion people as China, Russia, and India have entered the world economy, where is the dedicated sense of purpose to make the United States ready for a more competitive world?[14] Instead of mission and community, we have partisan politics carried out by ambitious egos.

> We need to regain our traditional spirit of optimism and the fierce competitiveness that makes us internally as well as externally competitive.

Great ideas are not abundant in the current political scene. No one is framing a vision of the future that we all want to happen. And, it is hard to remember the last time our political leaders had the courage and convictions to shape events and the determination and political savvy to make things happen. Too many politicians are too chicken or indecisive or partisan to create confidence in the public and enable this nation to create a sense of urgency for making the American Dream a continuing reality for us and future generations.

We need to regain our traditional spirit of optimism and the fierce competitiveness that makes us internally as well as externally competitive. In other words, we need to stop playing defense and let the offensive team onto the field.

The Psychological Recession has not only made American workers passive, it has also made the leaders of corporations excessively cautious.[15] Steve Hardis, who shared his corporate experiences in Chapter 10, recently commented that most corporations are very liquid now, but instead of using their cash to make large investments to create organic growth, they are doing financial engineering: strengthening their balance sheet, buying back shares, raising dividends, and making acquisitions. Too many technologies that were invented in the United States, like flat panels, HDTVs, and DVDs, are being brought to market by Asians.

The caution brought about by the pessimism inherent in the Psychological Recession is seen in executive decisions to look good financially through cutting costs and tinkering financially while avoiding market risk—and opportunity—by growing organically. For a capitalistic economy, this is very bad news: fear is winning.

Organizations cannot flourish and fulfill their possibilities when their leaders and their labor force are chronically scared. Fear destroys energy, trust, teamwork, innovation, and courage. This nation has to create an appropriate and effective safety net to help people cope with the shorter-term shifts in the economy, so that a greater sense of security will be a reality for everyone. Organizations must act on the premise that they have everything to gain by increasing their commitment to employees. And organizational boards will need to select leaders whose personal qualities include a belief in the American system, courage, integrity, and the fundamental optimistic sense that competition is just a spur toward greatness.

I recently saw two movies that fantasize—but also epitomize —the core values underlying the American Dream. *Rocky* (1976), the story of the rise of down-and-out Rocky Balboa who fights his way to become heavyweight champion of the world, and *Hoosiers* (1986), the story of a basketball team from a tiny high school in Indiana battling to become the state champions, and succeeding. The qualities that underlie the success of the underdog in both films are personal: a dogged, relentless sense that *I will never give up*, teamwork outweighing selfishness, self-reliance and discipline, and hope and faith in God or self or team. This mythology in fiction brings to life the opportunity and upward mobility that has been the reality for most Americans and the source of our optimism.

In the face of growing competition, it is imperative that we remember our basic values and rejoice in what we have accomplished in our brief history. From the courage of the immigrants to the guts of the pioneers who went West, the *"Can do!"* mantra of the Seabees in World War II and the vision that landed a man on the moon and created Silicon Valley, there is a legacy of courage and an entrepreneurial spirit in America.

Our basic traditions of wanting to make a difference, of ambition and confidence, of personal freedom and freedom of thought and of speech, of respect for individuals, and the view that the world is a meritocracy in which you are what you can achieve—these are the fundamental conditions that foster breakthrough thinking and innovation. And that's what will allow us to continue to succeed in a world that has become much smaller, flatter, and vastly more competitive.

Chapter 1

1. Hardis, Stephen, Personal Communication, February 4, 2003.
2. Kolker, Robert, "Down(sized) and Out in New York City," *New York*, March 17, 2003, pp. 23–28, and Brown, Ethan, "Generation HeXed," *New York*, March, 17, 2003, pp. 28–31.
3. Hilsenrath, Jon E., "Why for Many This Recovery Feels More Like a Recession," *The Wall Street Journal*, May 29, 2003, pp. A1 & 14.
4. Ibid.
5. Cooper, James C., "The Price of Efficiency," *Business Week*, March 22, 2004, pp. 38–42.
6. Hardis, Stephen Personal Communication, March 20, 2007.

Chapter 2

1. The 2001 recession began in the spring and ended in November of that year, according to the National Bureau of Economic Research.
2. Editorial page, "Media Bears," *The Wall Street Journal*, August 19, 2005, p. A12.
3. Ibid.

4. In the 2000 census, 56 percent of men and 43 percent of women aged 18 to 24 lived with one or both of their parents, a trend that has been increasing over the last 10 years. Yip, Pamela, "Hey, parents, we're home—again," *San Diego Union Tribune,* June 7, 2003, p. E12.

5. Crim, Dan and Seijts, Gerard H., "What engages employees the most, or, The Ten C's of employee engagement," *Ivey Business Journal,* March/April, 2006.

6. Tony DiRomualdo, Next Generation Consulting, as part of *The Future of Work* teleconference, March 31, 2005.

7. Futureofworkagenda@thefutureofwork.net, March 31, 2005, p. 3.

Chapter 3

1. Clifton, James K., "Engaging Your Employees: Six Keys to Understanding the New Workplace," "2002 SHRM Foundation Thought Leaders Remarks," *HR Society for Human Resource Management,* 2005, 6 pages. http://www.shrm.org/foundation/engaging.asp

2. Rucci, A.J., Kim, S.P., & Quinn, R.T., "The employee-customer-profit chain at Sears," *Harvard Business Review,* 76(1), 1998, pp. 82-98.

3. Serwer, Andy, "Hot Starbucks to Go," *Fortune,* January 26, 2004, pp. 60-74.

4. Kent, Steven, "Happy Workers Are the Best Workers," *The Wall Street Journal,* September 6, 2005, p. A20.

5. Rayburn, J. Mike, "The Impact of Downsizing," *Academy of Strategic and Organizational Leadership Journal,* 3(2), 1999, pp. 64-73.

6. Meyer, H., "Avoiding Pink Slips," *Nation's Business,* 1997, Volume 85, pp. 24-27.

7. (no author), "Heard Heigh-Ho, Heigh-Ho, It's Off to Work We Go, Lately?," *Corporate Board Member,* May/June 2003, pp. 42-46.

8. Kowalski, Bill, "Closing the Engagement Gap: Implications for Implementing Business Improvement Strategies," *Perspectives,* Workindex.com, 3 pages, 2003, on the web as http://www.workindex.com/editorial/hre/hre0301-special04.asp. The definition of discretionary effort comes from Daniel Yankelovich, the highly esteemed founder of the research and consulting firm that bears his name.

Chapter 4

1. Gordon, Joanne, "My Job, Myself, My Problem?" *Forbes.com,* 01.24.03, 7:00 AM ET, 3 pages. http://www.forbes.com/2003/01/24/cz_jg_0124work_print.html

2. Associated Press, "Fewer workers are happy with their job than in '90s," *San Diego Union Tribune*, March 1, 2005, p. C9.

3. (UK) AON Limited, "Pensions, Stress, Lack of Reward Cause Fall in Employee Commitment," *AON United Kingdom*, November 25, 2002, 3 pages. http://www.aon.com/uk/en/about/Press Office/nov25 *ukat-work.isp*

4. Hindo, Brian, Miles, John P., Grow, Brian, Arndt, Michaul, and Herbst, Moira, "The Customer: Satisfaction Not Guaranteed," *Business Week*, June 19, 2006, pp. 32–36.

5. Coombes, Andrea, "American workers not happy with jobs," *The San Diego Union-Tribune*, July 6, 2004, pp. C1 & 4.

6. Ibid.

7. Hanna, Nancy, "There's nothing 'soft' about productivity and commitment," *Ceridian Connection*, 2006, 2 pages. http://www.ceridian .com/myceridian/connection/article/printerfriendly/0,3123,13024-5856.

8. Dovale, Tony, "Riding the Razor," *Life Masters International*, 2005. http://lifemasters.co.zaDocs/ridingtherazor2.doc

9. Klassen, Hilary, "Engaging diversity, Engaging Employees: Achieving Diversity/Inclusiveness Goals," *The Gallup Organization*, 2005, 17 pages. http://72.12.203.104/search?q=cache:Nsic0QQQX0IJ:europa.eu.int/ comm/employment_soc

10. Woodcock, Neil, and Starkey, Michael, "CMAT (The Customer Management Scorecard), Engaging Employees to Deliver the Brand, State of the Nation IV: 2005," *QCI Assessment Ltd*, 2004, pp. 81–98. The estimates of turnover costs were based on an organization with 20,000 front-line employees with an average replacement cost of 0.41 percent of salary.

11. *Gallup* for Customer Loyalty Futures, June 2001. Note that the replacement cost would probably be considerably higher in 2006.

12. Counting the Costs: Absence and Labour Survey 2002, *CBI*, May 2002.

13. Klassen, *op cit.*

14. (no author), "Engagement: Increasing productivity by gaining the commitment of the workforce," no date. http://www.terranovatraining .co.uk/engagement.htm. Buckingham, Marcus, "Same indifference," *People Management*, February 17, 2000. Buckingham, Marcus, "What a waste," *People Management*, October 10, 2001, and Flade, Peter, "Great Britain's Workforce Lacks Inspiration," *Gallup Management*.

15. Buckingham, M., and Coffman, C., *First Break all the Rules* (New York: Simon & Schuster, 1999) and Corporate Leadership Council, "Driving Performance and Retention through employee engagement," Washington DC, 2004, and *Towers-Perrin*, "Working Today: Understanding What Drives Employee Engagement," 2003.

16. Crim and Seijts, *op cit*

17. Flade, Peter, "Great Britain's Workforce Lacks Inspiration," *Gallup Management Journal*, December 11, 2003, 3 pages. http://gmj.gallup.com/content/default.asp?ci=9847

18. Crim, Dan, and Seijts, Gerard H., "What engages employees the most, or, The Ten C's of employee engagement," *Ivey Business Journal*, March/April 2006.

19. Klassen, *op cit.*

20. Tritch, Teresa, "Engagement Drives Results at New Century," *Gallup Management Journal*, September 11, 2003, 4 pages. http://gmj.gallup.com/content/default.asp?ci.=1180.

Chapter 5

1. Fleming, John H., Coffman, Curt, and Harter, James K., "Manage Your Human Sigma," *Harvard Business Review*, July-August 2005, pp. 107–114.

2. Towers Perrin HR Services, "Working Today: Understanding What Drives Employee Engagement," *The Towers Perrin Talent report*, U.S. *Report*, 35 pages, charts on p. 20.

3. Woodcock, Neil and Starkey, Michael, Enterprise IG Case History for Customer Loyalty Futures UK, 8 July 2004.

4. Ibid.

5. Around the world, there is clearly great room for improvement because only 20 to 29 percent of employees are fully involved with their organization. The majority of workers are not engaged, and they destroy customer relationships at an annual cost of $300 billion a year in lost productivity.

6. Watson Wyatt Worldwide, *WorkUSA 2000*, "Employee Commitment and the Bottom Line, 2004, on the Web as http://www.watsonwyatt.com/europe/research/resrender.asp?id=W-304&page=2. Conchas, Edmundo, "Survey: Company profits tied to employee commitment": Watson Wyatt Global Consulting nationwide survey on attitudes, *2000 Dallas Business Journal*, March 10, 2000, http://www.bizjournals

.com/dallas/stories/2000/03/13/focus2.html. Schooley, Tim, "Study correlates investment value with management of 'human capital.' Happy employees translate into better stock performance," *Pittsburgh Business Times,* April; 7, 2000, 4 pages. On the Web as http://www. bizjournals.com/pittsburgh/stories/2000/04/10/focus4.html? jst=s_rs_hl

7. Fleming, Coffman and Harter, *op cit*

8. Royal, Carol, Daneshgar, Farhad, and O'Donnell, "Facilitating Organisational Sustainability Through Expert Investment Systems," *Academic Conferences Limited 2003* and *Electronic Journal on Knowledge Management,* 1(2) 2003, pp. 167–176. The HCI score is created by matching survey results and market value, the rate of return to share-holders, and Tobin's Q.

9. Watson Wyatt Worldwide research, *Human Capital Index: Linking Human Capital and Shareholder Value,* Watson Wyatt. 1–12. (2002)

10. Barber, L., Hayday S., and Bevan, S., "From People to Profits; the HR Link in the Service-Profit Chain," IES (the Institute for Employment Studies), Report 355, on the Web as http://employment-studies .co.uk/summary/summary.php?id=355, 4 pages, no date.

11. Holmes, Stanley, Zellner, Wendy, "US: Higher Wages Mean Higher Profits," *Business Week,* April 12, 2004, pp. 76–78.

12. Bary, Andrew, "Costco: More Gains Coming," *The Wall Street Journal,* in *The San Diego Union-Tribune,* February 18, 2007, p. H7.

13. Leggiere, Phil, "What Happened to the Leisure Society?," *Across the Board,* July/August 2002, p. 42–48, and an interview with SAS's CEO Goodnight on "60 Minutes," CBS, April 20, 2003.

14. (No author), "Heard Heigh-Ho, Heigh-Ho, It's Off to Work We Go Lately?," an interview with Best Company founder Robert Levering, and an interview with SAS's CEO James Goodnight on "60 Minutes," CBS, Sunday April 20, 2003, and *Across the Board,* July/August 2002, pp. 42–48.

15. Stark, M. "Five years of insight into the world's most admired com-panies," *Journal of Organizational Excellence,* 22(1) 2002, pp. 3–12.

16. Vanderbilt University and Hewitt Associates, 200. http://www .human-synergistics.com.au/content/articles/ezine/archive/2003-04/constructive_impact.htm

17. Dickler, Jessica, "Best employers, great returns," FORTUNE 100 Best Companies to Work For, *CNNMoney.com,* January 18, 2007. http://

money.cnn.com/2007/01/17/magazines/fortune/bestcompanies_
performance/index.htm

18. Hewitt and Associates, "Best Retainers of the Year," Survey, on Hewitt
    and Associates Website, http://was.hewitt.com/bestemployersaustralia/
    index.htm

19. Hewitt Associates, "Best Employers," *Hewitt quarterly Asia Pacific/
    Volume 3,* 2004, 3 pages. http://was4.hewitt.com/hewitt/ap/resource/
    rptspubs/hewittquart/HQ_10/best_employers.html

20. (no author) Heard Heigh-Ho, *op cit.*

21. Xilinx Media Fact Sheet QJFY06.pdf

22. Fox, Catherine, "Best Employers 2003," *Financial Review BOSS, 2002.*
    http://www.afrboss.com.au/magarticle.asp?doc_id=21489&listed_
    months=1

23. WfD Consulting, "The Business Case," WfD, *Consulting News and Events,*
    3 pages. http://www.wfd.com/news/bus_case.html

24. http://www.workfamily.com/Open/Pressreleases.htm.

25. Corporate Voices for Working Families, "Flexibility Is a Key
    Management Tool for the Workplace of the 21st Century," Press
    Release, November 8, 2005.

26. Bright Horizons Inc., "The real savings from employer-sponsored
    child care," Watertown MA.: Bright Horizons Inc. 2004. http://www
    .brighthorizons.com/investstudies/Investment%20Impact.FINAL
    .pdf

27. Landsman, L. "Juggling work and family," *Business Insurance,* 28(32),
    1994, p. 16.

28. Elswick, J., "More employers offer back-up child care," *Employee Benefit
    News,* 17(7). June 15, 2003. http://www.benefitnews.com/subscriber/
    Article.cfm?id=37881167

29. Ibid.

30. (UK) Dex, Shirley, and Smith, Colin, "Family-friendly employment
    policies 'matched by business success'," PressRoom, 2004. http://www
    .jrf.org.uk/pressroom/releases/270502.asp. (US) WfD Consulting,
    "The Business Case," WfD, *Consulting News and Events,* 3 pages. http://
    www.wfd.com/news/bus_case.html

31. Collins, J.C., and Porras, J.I. *Built to Last: Successful Habits of Visionary
    Companies.* rev. ed. (New York: *HarperBusiness,* 1994), and Collins, Jim,
    Good to Great: Why Some Companies Make the Leap, and Others Don't.
    (New York: *HarperBusiness,* 2001).

32. Hulbert, Mark, "Within Companies, Too, Education Proves Its Value," *The New York Times Company,* Copyright 2002, reprinted on the Web March 31, 2002.

33. *WatsonWyatt Worldwide, WorkUSA 2000,* "Employee Commitment and The Bottom Line," 2004. http://www.watsonwyatt.com/europe/ research/resrender.asp?id=W-304&page=2

34. *WorkUSA 2004/2005:* "Effective Employees Drive Financial Results," http://www.watsonwyatt.com/research/printable.asp?id=w_788.

35. Rosen, Corey, Case John, and Staubus, Martin, excerpted from *Why Employee Ownership Is Good for Business,* Harvard Business School Press, 2005, *Working Knowledge,* Harvard Business School, May 16, 2005, 6 pages.

36. Bevan, Stephen, Isles, Nick, Emery, Peter and Hopkins, Tony, "Achieving High Performance: CSR at the Heart of Business," The Work Foundation, *Virtuous Circle,* 2004.

37. Hewitt Associates, *op cit.*

38. Kronos Incorporated, "A CFO's Guide to Creating a High Performance Organization: Workforce Management Best Practices," July 2004.

Chapter 6

1. Personal communication, August 20, 2006. Professor Smarr is The Harry E. Gruber Professor, Department of Computer Science and Engineering at the University of California, San Diego. Dr. Smarr has been a pioneer in the development of the national information infra-structure: the Internet, the Web, the emerging Grid, collaboratories, and scientific visualization.

2. Advertisement for The Four Seasons Hotels & Resorts, *Wall Street Journal,* Feb. 16, 2007, p. A11.

3. The full interview with Steve Peltier was published as Chapter Two in Bardwick, Judith M., *In Praise of Good Business* (New York: John Wiley & Sons, 1998), pp. 20–31.

4. Beck, Cam, "The Meaning of Semper Fidelis." http://www.OO-rah .com/store/editorial/edi52.asp

5. While the birth dates for GenX and especially GenY are not as agreed upon as the dates for the Boomers, generally speaking the dates are 1946 to 1964 for the Boomers, 1961 to 1981 for GenX and 1982–2000 for GenY. http://en.wikipedia.org/wiki/generation, July 2006.

6. Ware, Jim, and Grantham, Charlie, "The Rise of the Emergent Worker," *The Future of Work Agenda,* April 1, 2006, pp. 9–12.

7. "Perfect Labor Storm," January 26, 2006. http://hrblog.typepad.com/perfect_labor_storm/2006/02/study_finds_hir.html

8. Lowenstein, Michael, "Cowboys and Saloons. Chicken and Eggs. Customers or Employees. Which came First?" CRMguru.com, Feb. 14, 2006, 5 pages. http://crmguru.custhelp.com/cgi-bin/crmguru.cfg/php/enduser/std_adp.php?p_faqid=1669

9. Ruth Anne Brown (name changed), personal communication June 21, 2006.

10. Recent data strongly suggest that the quality of the relationship between a customer and the organization is as significant as the one between an employee and the organization. When organizations ask customers, *"On a scale of one to ten, how likely is it that you would recommend us to your friends, colleagues, or clients,"* the answers were significant financially. When the responses of "detractors" (scores of 0–6) were subtracted from customers who were "promoters," (scores of 9–10), the resulting net promoter scores were closely correlated with the organization's revenue growth. McGregor, Jena, "Would You Recommend Us?," *Business Week,* January 30, 2006, pp. 94–95.

Chapter 7

1. Disgruntled Employees: Gordon, Joanne: "My Job, Myself, My Problem?" *Forbes.com,* January 24, 2003, referencing the 2003 Towers-Perrin Study.

2. Frolik, Joe, "Pulling together in a labor of trust," *Forum, The Plain Dealer,* July 9, 2006, p. H1 & 3.

3. Levering, Robert and Moskowitz, Milton, "100 Best Companies to Work For, Large Companies" *Fortune,* January 24, 2006 pp. 72–78.

4. Hardis, Stephen, Personal communication, July 17, 2005.

5. Hymowitz, Carol, "Middle Managers Are Unsung Heroes on Corporate Stage," *The Wall Street Journal,* September 19, 2005, p. B1.

6. Ibid.

7. Bardwick, Judith M., first published in Gray, General Al, USMA (Ret.) and Otte, Dr. Paul, *The Conflicted Leader and Vantage Leadership* (Columbus, OH: Franklin University Press, 2006), Foreword, p. v.

8. We owe General Al Gray USMC (Ret.) and Dr. Paul Otte great thanks for bringing us a very clear and convincing description of the U.S.

military's and especially the U.S. Marine Corps extraordinary success in creating leaders and a culture of leadership throughout the organization.

Chapter 8

1. WatsonWyatt Worldwide *WorkUSA 2000—Employee Commitment and the Bottom Line*© 2006, 2 pgs., For more information visit www.watsonwyatt.com. http://www.watsonwyatt.com/europe/research/resrender.asp?id=W-304&page=6
2. Bardwick, Judith M., *The Plateauing Trap* (New York: AMACOM, 1986).

Chapter 9

1. "Perfect Labor Storm," January 26, 2006. http://hrblog.typepad.com/perfect_labor_storm/2006/02/stydy_finds_hir.html
2. Greene, Jay and France, Mike, "Culture Wars Hit Corporate America," *BusinessWeek,* May 23, 2005, pp. 90–93.
3. Tables 1 and 2 were initially published in Bardwick, Judith M., *Seeking the Calm in the Storm* (NJ: Financial Times Prentice Hall, 2002), 216–217.

Chapter 10

1. Personal communication, interview with Stephen Hardis, CEO of Eaton Corporation from 1995 to 2000, interviewed on October 22, 2005, Cleveland, OH.

Chapter 11

1. Krugman, Paul, "Economic boom not benefiting most," *The New York Times,* reprinted in *The San Diego Union-Tribune,* December 6, 2005, p. B7.
2. (editorial), "Good Jobs at Good Wages," *The Wall Street Journal,* July 11, 2006.
3. Hall, Kevin G., "For many, outlook not so rosy," *The San Diego Union-Tribune,* May 10, 2006, pp. C1 & 4.
4. Crutsinger, Martin, "Productivity slows while wages post increase," *The San Diego Union-Tribune,"* September 7, 2006, p. C4.
5. Brown, Peter A., "In real world, wealth is shared unevenly," *The San Diego Union Tribune,* April 25, 2006, p. B7.
6. Conkey, Christopher, "Jobs Data Keep Economic Optimists Smiling," *The Wall Street Journal,* December 9–10, 2006, p. A3.

7. (editorial), "Tales from the Crypt," *The Wall Street Journal,* September 29, 2006, p. A16.

8. Samuelson, Robert J., "Instability in a stable U.S. economy," *Newsweek,* February 15, 2006, p. B8.

9. Brooks, David, "Populist myths on income inequality," *The New York Times,* reprinted in *The San Diego Union-Tribune,* September 8, 2006. p. B8.

10. Ibid.

11. Reynolds, Alan, "The Top 1% . . . of What?" *The Wall Street Journal,* December 14, 2006, p. A20.

12. Crabtree, Penni, "Good old days gone for biotech," *The San Diego Union-Tribune,* November 26, 2006, pp. A1 & 16.

13. Etter, Lauren, "Labor Day: A Report Card for American Workers," *The Wall Street Journal,* September 2, 2006, p. A7.

14. (editorial), "Rodney Dangerfield Revisited," *The Wall Street Journal,* December 30, 2005, p. A16, and Shiller, Robert J., "The rising wealth of nations," *The San Diego Union Tribune,* December 10, 2006, p. G6.

15. Etter, Lauren, *Op Cit.*

16. Brooks, David, *Op Cit.*

17. (editorial) Dangerfield and Shiller, *Op Cit.*

18. Hubbard, Glenn, R., "Hidden Treasury," *The Wall Street Journal,* June 5, 2006, p. A11.

19. Will, George F., "Labor unions for the 21st century," *The San Diego Union-Tribune,* December 29, 2005, p. B10.

20. I disagree a bit with Mayor Bloomberg because I think that description applies to the Big Three auto makers thus far in the twenty-first as well as the twentieth centuries. Bloomberg, Michael R., "Flabby, Inefficient, Outdates," *The Wall Street Journal,* December 14, 2006, p. A20.

21. Wong, Nicole C., "HP hires workers as it lets other go," *San Jose Mercury News,* reprinted in the *San Diego Union Tribune,* December 26, 2006. pp. C1 and 3.

22. (editorial), "The European Disease," *The Wall Street Journal,* February 8, 2006, p. A16.

23. Ibid.

24. Wright, Tom, "Indonesia's Labor Laws Deter," *The Wall Street Journal,* December 7, 2006, p. A8.

25. Sundquist, Bruce, "Globalization: The Outsourcing-Insourcing Issue," Edition 2, June 2006, 7 pages. http://home.alltel.net/bsundquist1/ins.html.

26. Offshore Outsourcing World Staff, "Insourced Jobs Pay More," *Offshore Outsourcing World,* October 25, 2004, 3 pages. http://www .enterblog.com/200410250656.html

27. Kane, Tim, Hederman, Rea S., and Johnson, Kirk, "Framing the Economic Debate," WebMemo #582, The Heritage Foundation. http://www.heritage.org/Research/Economy/wm582.cfm.

28. The Bureau of Labor publishes this data as "U-4," the rate of discouraged and underemployed people. Cited in Kane, Tim, *op cit.*

29. (editorial), "Good Jobs at Good Wages," *op cit.*

30. (editorial), "Good Jobs at Good Wages," *op cit.*

31. Kane, Tim, *op cit.*

32. Kimmitt, Robert M., "Job Changes Strengthen the U.S. Economy," *The San Diego Union-Tribune,* January 24, 2007, p. B7.

33. Pethokoukis, James M., "Anxiety Attack," *U.S. News & World Report,* June 26, 2006, pp. 42–45.

34. Lublin, Joann S., Zimmerman, Ann, and Terhune, Chad, "Behind Nardelli's Abrupt Exit," *The Wall Street Journal,* January 4, 2007, pp. A1 and 12. In 2000, Jill Barad left Mattel with a $50 million package.[32] In 2005, Philip Purcell was forced out of Morgan Stanley with a $62 million pay package, and Carly Fiorina departed Hewlett-Packard with "only" $21 million. Tom Preston exited Viacom with $59 million, and Henry McKinnel of Pfizer got the grand prize of $200 million. That package was eclipsed in 2007 when Robert Nardelli was fired from Home Depot and exited with a package worth $210 million.

Chapter 12

1. Industries and communities can also experience catastrophic competitive crises but the data appear to overwhelmingly support the view that government interventions generally have far worse consequences than letting the free market make decisions.

2. Brooks, Arthur C., "Who Cares about the Poor?," *The Wall Street Journal,* January 24, 2007, p. A13.

3. Bardwick, Judith M., *Danger in the Comfort Zone,* (New York: AMA-COM, 1991 and 1995) (updated paperback edition).

4. Nathan, Joe, "True Charter School Idea Embodies Basic American Principles," *The Wall Street Journal,* "Letters to the Editor," January 21, 207, p. A6.

5. Parker, Star, "A lesson in education from Oprah," *Scripps Howard News Service,* reprinted in *The San Diego Union-Tribune,* January 6, 2007, p. B8.

6. Nathan, Joe, *op cit.*

7. Henninger, Daniel, "Give Top Teachers a Bonus," *The Wall Street Journal,* January 19, 2007, p. A14.

8. Nathan, Joe, *op cit.*

9. Kondrake, Morton, "Needed: A radical change in schools," Roll Call, reprinted in *The San Diego Union-Tribune,* December 29, 2006, p. B8.

10. Solomon, Deborah, and Wessel, David, "Health-Insurance Gap Surges as Political Issue," *The Wall Street Journal,* January 19, 2007, pp. A1 and 12.

11. Zhang, Jane, and Lueck, Sarah, "Bush Health Plan Shifts Onus to the Consumer," *The Wall Street Journal,* January 25, 2007, p. A6.

12. Associated Press, "Benefits larger part of worker pay," *The San Diego Union-Tribune,* January 8, 2007, p. C5.

13. Lahart, Justin, "Rethinking Health Care and the GDP," *The Wall Street Journal,"* January 25, 2007, p. C1.

14. (editorial page), "Illegal Health Care," *The Wall Street Journal,* January 23, 2007, p. A18. It seems likely that the plans put forth by states that require employers to participate in the state's healthcare system or pay a penalty are illegal because they violate a federal employee benefits law known as Erisa. A 2006 ruling by the Fourth Circuit Court of Appeals held that Maryland's new employee healthcare law violated Erisa's basic purpose of allowing businesses that operate in multiple states to have nationwide health and other benefit plans.

15. (editorial page), "Health and Taxes," *The Wall Street Journal,* January 24, 2007, p. A12.

16. Ibid.

17. Emanuel, Ezekiel, and Fuchs, Victor, "How to Cure U.S. Health Care," *Fortune,* November 13, 2006, p. 78.

18. Stanley Holmes, "Into the Wild Blog Yonder," *Business Week,* May 22, 2006, pp. 84–86.

19. Jane C. Linder, "Continuous Renewal: Managing for the Upside." *US Business Review,* October 2005, 5 pages. http://www.usbusinessreview.com/content_archives/Oct05/04.html.

20. Barry Rubin and Richard Rubin, "Labor-Management Partnerships: A New Approach to Collaborative Management." Pricewaterhouse Coopers Human Capital Series, July 2001, 34 pages.

21. Will, George F., "What a difference five decades make," *The Washington Post,* reprinted in *The San Diego Union-Tribune,* November 26, 2006, p. G2.

22. Eckel, Russ, "Feature Article: Who Let Detroit Burn?," *Future of Work Agenda,* July 5, 2006, pp. 6–8.

23. Ibid.

24. Whitehouse, Mark, "For Some Manufacturers, There Are Benefits to Keeping Production at Home," *The Wall Street Journal,* January 22, 1007, p. A2.

25. Bloomberg News, "Costco, union have tentative pact," *The San Diego Union-Tribune,* January 24, 2007, p. A11.

26. All starred items are in Pethokoukis, James, M., "Anxiety Attack," *U.S. News & World Report,* June 26, 2006, pp. 42–45. Many starred items were first suggested by Gene Sperling, President Clinton's director of the National Economic Council from 1996 to 2001. His ideas are described more fully in his book, *The Pro-Growth Progressive,* (New York: Simon & Schuster, 2005).

27. In 2007, there is strong bipartisan support in Congress for an increase in the minimum wage from $5.15 to $7.25 an hour, which many economists oppose.

28. Health savings accounts are very useful for people whose health insurance includes high deductibles. In these plans pretax money can be invested and funds can be withdrawn tax-free to pay medical costs.

Chapter 13

1. The period was brilliantly described and analyzed in Morris, Charles R., "Freakoutonomics," *The New York Times,* June 2, 2006, OP-ED, Section A, p. 21.

2. CSPP, "Offshore Outsourcing: Myths and Realities," 4 pages, no date www.techceocouncil.og/documents/Ten_Common_Myths_about_w orldwide_sourcing.pdf.

3. Malpass, David, "Fed-Side Manner," *The Wall Street Journal,* May 11, 2006, p. A18.

4. Ewing, Peter, "Income Inequality Inspires Achievement and Success," *The Wall Street Journal,* "Letters to the Editor," September 12, 2006, p. A2.

5. (no author), "America's Pursuit of Happiness," *The Economist,* reprinted in the *The San Diego Union-Tribune,* July 2, 2006, p. G6.

6. Samuelson, Robert J., "America's competitiveness panic," *Newsweek,* reprinted in the *The San Diego Union-Tribune,* August 10, 2006, p. B10.

7. Zakaria, Fareed, "How Long Will America Rule the World?," *Newsweek,* June 12, 2006, pp. 40–45.

8. Associated Press, "Immigrants play major role in tech startups," *The San Diego Union-Tribune,* January 4, 2007, p. C4.

9. Friedman, Thomas, "Anxiety over education goes global," *The New York Times,* reprinted in the *The San Diego Union-Tribune,* March 25, 2006, p. B8.

10. Brooks, David, "Score one for U.S. universities," *The New York Times,* reprinted in the *The San Diego Union Tribune,* June 23, 2006, p. B8.

11. Zakaria, Fareed, *op cit.*

12. Cox, Christopher, "The SEC Can Help Russia," *The Wall Street Journal,* July 11, 2006, p. A12.

13. Matthews, Robert Guy, "U.S. Is Ranked Leader in business Innovation," *Wall Street Journal,* January 16, 2007, p. A19. In 2006, INSEAD, a prominent business school near Paris analyzed and ranked 107 countries and published its findings in 2007. The United States is by far the most innovating country in the world, and American corporate spending on R&D is vastly greater than that of any other country.

14. Gergen, David, "Great to Good?," *U.S. News & World Report,* June 26, 2006, p. 72.

15. Hardis, Stephen R., Personal Communication, March 28, 2006.

Unemployment (*continued*)
economy and, 148–149
perception of, 156–157
Psychological Recession and, 15, 19
Unions. *See also* Organized labor
decline of, 150, 184
downsizing and, 32
Eaton and, 130, 134
employee satisfaction and, 22–23
productivity and, 136
Psychological Recession and, 15
United Auto Workers (UAW), 130, 134, 183
United Steelworkers, 81
University of Michigan, 103–104

V
Values
Best Fit and, 114–115
as competitive advantage, 145
individualism and, 195–196
VAT (value added tax), 178–179
Verizon Communications, 152
Vivaldi, 49
Volatility, 149

W
Wages. *See also* Compensation; Salaries
competition and, 4
Costco and, 51–52
GDP and, 150
increases in, 148

perception of, 158
Wakefield School, 170–171
The Wall Street Journal, 5
Wal-Mart, 15, 51–52, 185. *See also* Sam's Club
Watson Wyatt, 50–51, 59
WEF. *See* World Economic Forum
Welch, Jack, 87
Westinghouse, 183–184
WFC Resources. *See* Work & Family Connection
Wiefek, Nancy, 159
Work & Family Connection, 57
"Working Today: Exploring Employees' Emotional Connection to Their Jobs," 36
Work-life balance, 67–68
Workplace, humanizing, 95–97
Work trends, 22
WorkUSA study, 59
Work weeks, compressed, 57
WorldCom, 153
World Economic Forum (WEF), 149
World War II, 1–2
Seabees and, 202
wage controls in, 173

X
Xerox, 2
Xilinx, 55

Y
Yahoo, 39